MW01491657

Patrick Cahill 1848-1931
Father, Businessman, Explorer

Rough Weather All Day

An Account of
the "Jeannette" Search Expedition
from Log Kept by Patrick Cahill
Machinist on Board
U. S. S. "Rodgers"

— edited by —

David Hirzel

for my mother Irene Doris Hirzel
in small token of my love and respect

* * *

* * *

Other works by David Hirzel (available through Terra Nova Press):
Sea Sonnets (2009)
Sailor on Ice: Tom Crean with Scott in the Antarctic 1910-1913 (2011)
Hold Fast: Tom Crean with Shackelton's *Endurance* Expedition 1913-1917 (2013)

Cover image by iStockphoto

U.S.S. Rodgers

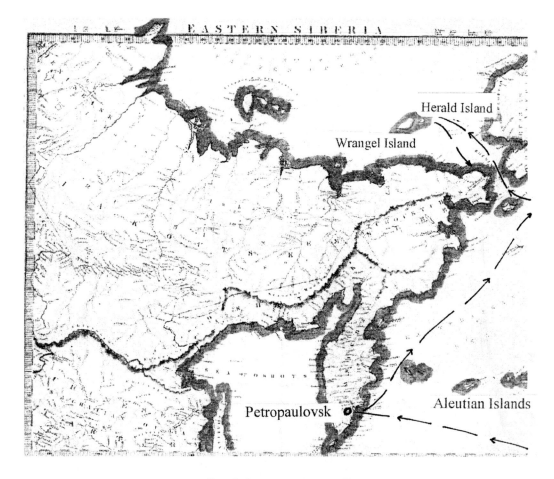

Track of the *U.S.S. Rodgers*

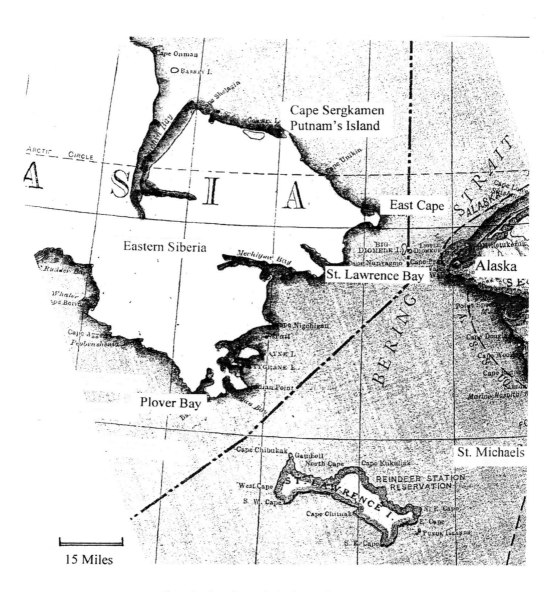

Eastern Siberia in the vicinity of St. Lawrence Bay

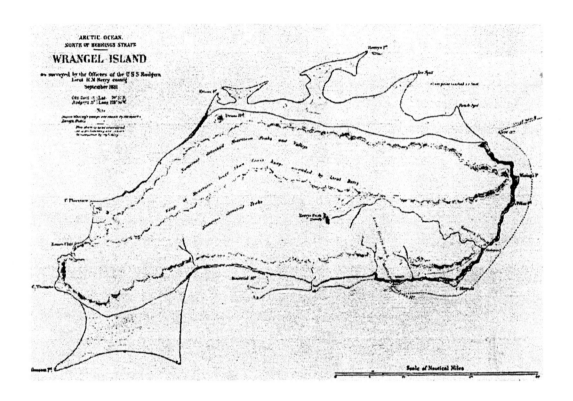

Survey Map of Wrangel Island
by the Officers of *U.S.S. Rodgers*

Table of Contents

Table of Contents..11

Introduction...13

Editorial Note...19

1. The Start of the Expedition...21

2. Preparation..25

3. Departure..29

4. Into the Arctic..43

5. The Arctic Whalers..57

6. Shore Station on Cape Sergkaman..65

7. Preparing to Winter at St. Lawrence Bay...............................71

8. Fire!...85

9. Settling Into the Villages...103

10. Life Among the Natives at St. Lawrence Bay, Siberian Coast,
   Russian Province, Asia..109

11. Scurvy..131

12. Rescue..141

Appendix One: Capt. Berry's Inland Trip at Wrangel Island
   August-September 1881..151

Appendix Two: Mr. Waring's Trip Sailing East at Wrangel Island
   August-September 1881..157

Appendix Three: Ensign Hunt's Trip Sailing West on the Coast of
   Wrangel Island 1881 August-September 1881.........................161

Glossary...169

Introduction

By the year 1880, the United States Navy was in the middle of its long transition from sail power to steam. On board the ships at sea, the seamen tended to the ship on deck, the stokers kept the fires burning hot, but it was the Engineering Department who kept the whole business going day and night, through every watch, from port to port. After only two years in the service, Patrick Cahill had risen quickly to the rank of Machinist's Mate. In the Brooklyn Navy Yard he had full access to the resources necessary to the maintenance of the steam engines that were taking over the place of sail in the ships of the modern navy.

Patrick Cahill was born February 1848 in County Cork, Ireland, and was brought to the United States as a very young child in 1850. Nothing is known of his early life, but he must have been fascinated as many young men were with the power and speed of the steam locomotives of the growing railroad systems. In 1874 he left the noise and bustle of the city for the lush jungles of Central America, taking a job with the Panama Railway. There he first began to realize not only his true calling in the steam driven world of industry, but also his sense of justice in the world of men. When he saw the way the priests in the Catholic Church in Panama treated the native Americans there with contempt and disdain, he renounced the church entirely. After four years working on the railway Cahill left the heat and humidity, the squalor and poverty of Panama for the cooler climate and better prospects of Boston, Massachusetts. He secured employment as a mechanic and then met and married Miss Emma Frances Small, a proper Bostonian, small of stature and sweet, in sharp contrast to his large frame and short hot temper. Together they raised four children—Wendell Eldridge, Starr, Sumner Edison, and Alma Rebecca—in the Unitarian faith.

By the spring of 1880, Cahill had put his mechanical skills to better use in the United States Navy. It was a time of peace; there had been no substantial martial activity since the conclusion of the War Between the States. The ships now in use were largely propelled by steam, although most of them still carried sail just in case the developing technology of steam propulsion failed to live up to its promise. The steam engines of the modern Navy's ships were complicated affairs, prone to minor disturbances of function that will require the patient hand of a specialist—the Machinist's Mate. This warrant officer may be called upon do almost anything in the service of these machines. When their moving parts—there are hundreds of them—go out of adjustment he brings them back into near-perfect alignment. When they break apart from metal fatigue, he forges replacements right on board the ship. Oiling, valve adjustment, mending, rebuilding: the Machinist's Mate is always ready. He has to be.

It requires a great deal of ingenuity. And patience. Not every man was up for the post, but Patrick Cahill had found his place in the hierarchy of the service. In truth, it made few demands on his intellect, and offered few inducements to his innate sense of adventure. His chosen career path offered only so much chance of advancement, and no more. He had gone about as high as a man with his background and limited education could expect to rise.

A new opportunity beckoned—the fascination, the lure of the unknown Arctic is taking the nation by storm. Newspapermen, among them James Gordon Bennett, owner of the *New York Herald*, sell papers in part by stirring up exciting news rife with danger, human suffering, and heroism. Few stories can combine these concepts more successfully than the real-life adventures of Arctic exploration. The tragic loss in 1842 of Sir John Franklin's entire expedition in the Northwest Passage had all the right ingredients to capture the interest of the reading public for decades. By the late 1870s that interest was looking toward new adventures, and the "conquest" of the North Pole.

Bennett commissioned a ship, the *Jeannette,* with just that task: to sail to that imaginary spot at the axis of our Earth, come home and tell the world—or the readers of the *New York Herald* at any rate—just what was to be found there. She departed San Francisco on July 8, 1879, with a full crew of Navy volunteers, bound through the Bering Strait into the Arctic Ocean, then westward to Wrangel Island above Siberia. From that remote outpost she was to sail northward to the Pole. She sailed instead into oblivion.

It was no unusual thing in those days long before the advent of ship-to-shore radio, for a vessel to be out of touch entirely with the rest of the world for extended periods of time. In the case of polar exploration, years could pass as they had with Franklin, where no communication was nothing to worry about. But when by the spring of 1880 no word of "all well" had been sent home by a passing whaler, the U.S. Navy began to worry about the missing *Jeannette*.

The time had come to go north in search of her. Another sailing vessel was purchased and strengthened for the ice, to be manned by young sailors in search of a new adventure. When word passed through the Navy seeking volunteers for this hazardous Arctic duty, Patrick Cahill answered the call. A new steam whaler with "a great spread of sail," the *Mary and Helen* been purchased and then further strengthened for work in the polar ice at the Navy's west coast shipyard at Mare Island in California. She was bark-rigged, length one hundred fifty-five feet, beam thirty feet. Renamed the *U.S.S. Rodgers*, she would need that canvas. For a new ship, her engines would turn out to be a constant source of trouble for the

Machinist's Mate.

No one knew as yet that their venture, and the *Jeannette*—the object of their search—were already doomed. The missing ship had been trapped in the sea ice in the Arctic Ocean off Herald Island since September 6, 1879. She was in May of 1881 still afloat, although damaged, carried by the drift and current to a new "farthest north." It was an honor most of her men would never survive long enough to claim. No one knew just where she was, but the *Rodgers* was going to find out.

Along with most of the crew, Cahill volunteered for the expedition the Receiving Ship at the Brooklyn Navy Yard. They came west on the *U.S.S. Independence* and on May 30. 1881 joined their new ship at the Mare Island Navy Yard in Vallejo, California. The expedition left San Francisco amid considerable fanfare on June 16, bound on their heroic mission.

The voyage of the *Rodgers* never succeeded in its goals. No trace of the *Jeannette* was to be found. Dense ice pack blocked the way North and prevented any exploring or discovery in that direction. While the *Rodgers* did reach and chart the coast of Wrangel Island a hundred miles north of the Siberian coastline, hers was not the first American expedition to do so. The revenue cutter *U.S.S. Corwin* with John Muir aboard reached those shores a few weeks earlier and left behind records of her visit.

Before leaving Cahill contracted with the *San Francisco Chronicle* to act as its correspondent during the voyage, providing him with paper, pens, and an order to use telegraph if necessary if necessary. "I explained that I had never tried this kind of work, but agreed to do so if anything worth recording happened," he writes in his log. Although Cahill kept daily notes of the doings in and about his ship, he makes no mention of sending any of them home via telegraph or passing ship. Evidently these notes did not make it to the States before he did. They remained instead in rough manuscript form, to be later transcribed by a typist into the manuscript that is the basis of Rough Weather All Day. Patrick Cahill's log, like a ship's log, recounts the events of every day in succession, without fail, regardless of whether the events of a given day are tumultuous—such as the day the ship burned to the waterline—or mundane. In either case, he is never short on details, and it is in those details, in his wry commentaries and acerbic observations on the foibles of his fellow survivors that the true charm of his narrative comes through.

The *Rodgers* stopped first at Port Petropaulovsk in Russian Kamchatka and next at the government station at St. Michaels in Alaska. Her next port of call, if it could be called such, was the whalers' rendezvous at Plover Bay, and after that St. Lawrence Bay in far eastern Siberia. It was not until August 22nd, that she cleared the Bering Strait and headed west along the northern coast of Siberia on her mission to learn the fate of the *Jeannette*. Despite Cahill's patient care with what had been a brand new ship, the boilers and steam engines were always on the verge of breakdown and in constant need of repair.

The *Rodgers* retraced the track of that doomed ship, calling in her wake first at Herald Island, but found no trace of her. In the course of the search the men of the *Rodgers* first charted and explored the desolate shores of Wrangel Island. Along the way they encountered the aboriginal natives of far northern Siberia, and got to know them intimately, more perhaps than they would have liked.

With winter closing in and still no sign of the lost *Jeannette,* Cahill's ship retreated back along the coast, leaving a party under Sailing Master Charles Putnam at Sergkaman Bay before calling again at St. Lawrence Bay to take up winter quarters. There, in the early morning of November 30th, disaster struck. "At 8:45 A.M. smoke came up the pipe from the chain locker, and Morgan went aft and reported the ship on fire in the forehold . . . the fire pumps had been disconnected to keep them from freezing." By the end of the day the ship was burned to the waterline. All the men were safely ashore, with the few supplies they were able to salvage. They would be spending the winter as the forced guests of the natives, a genuine culture shock to both sides of the arrangement.

Neither the host peoples nor their uninvited guests were prepared for their sudden enforced cohabitation, but both sides made the best of it. The native Tchoutkichi people—"Chook-Chees" to the sailors—lived in low hide-covered huts gathered into small isolated villages scattered around the barren land of far-eastern Siberia. For centuries they had managed a subsistence level existence on the meager resources of the land and sea. Starvation was a constant threat through the long harsh winters, when the scarce game was barely enough to sustain their own population. Now they were expected, and willing, to share what little they had in food and shelter with thirty-six American seamen and their Russian dog-driver.

There was not enough of either to go around. The men crowded into the existing "yoronger" huts in four isolated villages, making their beds the cramped quarters amid the squalor and enforced intimacy of family life in huts too small in floor plan to accommodate everyone, and too low to stand up in. There were fights, and deaths. The threat of starvation was a constant companion throughout the winter. Cahill contracted and nearly died from scurvy, but he never stopped keeping his daily record of the events and people around him. That record is the source and foundation of this book.

Cahill did survive, as did his narrative. In the spring of 1882 a whaler coming north to the Bering fishery for the season found the stranded sailors and brought them off. Returned to San Francisco on June 23rd 1882, Cahill recovered from his near-death from scurvy. He paid off in Brooklyn, left the Navy, and returned with his family to take up a new life in California. Putting his machinist's skills to good use, he found employment with the growing cable-car lines of San Francisco. Later he made a career for himself in the commercial elevator business, founding the firm Cahill and Hall Elevator Company. Patrick and Emma Cahill took up residence in a large home at 1030 56th Street in Oakland. Their grandchildren remembered two large suits of medieval armor standing in the foyer to greet visitors, and elaborate birthday parties around a centerpiece of American flags. Emma Cahill started a school milk program and was one of the founders of the Oakland PTA.

Forty-two years after the event, Cahill found himself in the limelight again when journalist George C. Henderson of the Oakland Tribune settled him in for an extended interview to enlarge upon his experiences as an Arctic explorer on board the *U. S. S. Rodgers*. His recollections as reported in the paper sometimes seem more elaborate than the words of his diary kept in the field.

Portions of that series have been interwoven here with his log of daily events written in the moment. His recollections quoted by the reporter included events and conversations that never made it into his own written narrative. The editor of this volume <u>Rough Weather All Day</u> can only suppose that Cahill's story, retold forty years on by a voluble Irishman to a credulous reporter with a mission to sell more newspapers, ended up in print with considerable embellishment. How else to explain these words about Wrangel Island from the *Tribune* story: "The crevices were thick with gold that had been washed down by the melting snow. Members of the crew gathered it in cans." Those who are recalled as having plans to go back to the island again someday for the riches, never did.

The two accounts, brought together in this volume, bring to life a story that has never before been told. There are no great acts of compelling heroism, just the small acts that comprise the lives of ordinary men who, cast away on desperate shores, want only to come home. They find themselves the uninvited guests of other ordinary people, who in their way do everything they can to help. In the mix of disparate civilizations, moments of humor, generosity, tragedy and terror shine in the unadorned prose of Patrick Cahill.

After an adventurous and prosperous life Cahill, "a fine gentleman," died in 1931 after a long illness. His legacy, of course, continues in the lives of his descendants. Their generosity in providing this manuscript now shares his adventure with all those who seek the true, as yet unheralded, stories of Arctic adventure.

Editorial Note

The transcription of the manuscript text follows the typewritten original with the following exceptions:

1. The punctuation has been modified in that some long strings of independent clauses joined there by semicolons have been broken up into shorter sentences at the discretion of the editor. Many of the strings of independent clauses have been retained, as will be evident.

2. Spelling of place names and Siberian given names has been regularized for consistency. Place names are given in the form in which Cahill knew them. Some of the native settlements cannot be identified with modern place names, and are likely to have disappeared altogether with the passage of time. Place name spellings (e.g. "Wrangle," "Wrangel," "Wrangell") appear as given in the various publications from which they are quoted.

3. Where appropriate the archaic or misinformed spelling of common words has been corrected to modern usage, e.g. Cahill's "*dingy*" (a small ship's boat) has been corrected to "*dinghy*."

4. The original idiosyncratic capitalization, spelling and punctuation have otherwise been retained. It is not clear whether these have arisen directly from Cahill, or are the work of his unnamed typist. In either case they lend an air of authenticity to his story that might otherwise be lost.

5. Occasionally a word has been added in brackets to clarify Cahill's seamanlike colloquial usage, as in "[sick] bay." Editorial comments with

no reference citations are also indicated by enclosure in brackets.

Excerpts or notes from the following works have been inserted where appropriate into the transcription of Cahill's manuscript. Such insertions will be designated by an indentation of the entire passage, introduced by the source in brackets italic *[Source]* and concluded with a reference to between —dashes—.

The *Oakland Tribune* ran a three-week Sunday special series based on interviews with Cahill taken in about 1922. Portions of this series have been paraphrased to enliven the manuscript and illustrate aspects of the expedition that did not originally appear in it. Some of the excerpts from the *Tribune* piece are accurately dated (that is, the dates agree with Cahill's manuscript), some are not, some are not dated at all. Portions of it are quoted without attribution, others have no parallel in the manuscript so we assume that these tales were taken in interview.

Notes from the narrative of the revenue cutter *U.S.S. Corwin* during her visit to Wrangel Island, and that portion of her voyage in 1882 in which the survivors from the *Rodgers* returned home to the United States.

Excerpts taken from Our Lost Explorers: The Narrative of the *Jeannette* Arctic Expedition edited by Raymond Lee Newcomb (American Publishing Company, Hartford 1888)

Excerpts from "Arctic Expeditions—The *Jeannette*, the *Rodgers*, and the *Alliance*," from the *Annual Report of the Secretary of the Navy, November 28, 1881*. (Washington, DC: US Government Printing Office, 1881)

1. The Start of the Expedition

Here begins
An Account of the Jeanette Search Expedition
from Log Kept by Patrick Cahill
Machinist on Board U. S. S. "Rodgers"
[in his own words]

In the spring of 1881, after the people and press of the whole Country had been agitating for a relief part to go in search of the Arctic Exploring Steamer "Jeannette," Captain De Long commanding, also the whale ships "Vigilant" and "Mount Wolloston," the United States Government appropriated a sum of money to defray the expenses of a ship and provisions. Said ship was to be in charge of the United States Navy Department.

The Officers received their appointments and orders to report for duty at San Francisco, California.

The Vessel selected for service was the Steam Whaler Barque, "Mary and Helen." The name of this vessel was changed to "RODGERS."

After a survey by the Government Officials, she was ordered to Mare Island Navy Yard, to be fitted out and provisioned for a three-year cruise. As the vessel was expected to go in the ice, her bow was fitted with a heavy composition Ice Breaker and the hull was lined with heavy sheathing. Additional Cabin and Bunks were put in and the vessel was well fitted out and plenty of good provisions and clothing taken on board.

When the call was issued for Volunteers for the crew, more than two hundred already in the United States Navy were examined, and from this number twenty-five men were selected; as severe duty was required and to be expected, the men selected were in the best physical and mental condition. All were between the ages of twenty-three and thirty-five years; weight of the men was to be from 2-1/4 to 2-1/2 pounds for each inch in height. Most of them had been in the service and knew what was to be expected of them. All were ordered to report on the Receiving Ship at the Brooklyn Navy Yard, were they signed for the cruise of the "Rodgers." Lieut. Lamberton took the crew from the Brooklyn Navy Yard and turned them over to the officers of the Mare Island Yard. From the "Independence" we went on board the "Rodgers" for duty.

Three of the crew deserted during the time we were in San Francisco Bay. They were replaced by men from the U.S.S. "Pensacola." Eight different nationalities were represented in this crew and then United States Ships gave the full number.

When all Officers, men and stores were aboard we came down from Mare Island Yard to San Francisco Bay, where final orders were received. On the 16th day of June we sailed for the Arctic amid cheering, firing salutes, blowing whistles, etc. Several Government Tugs accompanied us to the Heads.

The following are the Officers and Crew answering to Roll Call on United States Steamer "Rodgers."

JEANETTE SEARCH EXPEDITION

Lieutenant Robert M. Berry, Commanding U.S.S. "Rodgers" of the Jeanette Search Expedition.

Howard Scott Waring, Master U.S.N. Executive Officer and Navigator.

Dr. Meredith Dabney Jones, U.S.N., Past Assistant Surgeon.

Master Charles. F. Putnam, U.S.N., came aboard to take the place of Wm. F. Halsey, W.S.N, who was unfit for the voyage on account of a big Spree and its results; he was sent ashore.

Abraham V. Zane, U.S.N., Past Assistant Engineer.

Henry Jackson Hunt, U.S.N., Ensign.

George Middleton Stoney, J.S.N., Ensign.

Dr. Joaquin D. Castillo, U.S.N., Assistant Surgeon.

Col. W. H. Gilder, Pay Clerk and Correspondent for the New York Herald. He had seen service in the Arctic, having been with Swartzka's Expedition to King William's Land.

Herbert T. De Tracey, Acting Carpenter U.S.N.

Scoby Willard Morrison, 1st Class Machinist U.S.N.

George Gardener, 1st Class Machinist U.S.N.

Patrick Cahill, 1st Class Machinist U.S.N.

Joseph Hodgson, Paymaster's Yeoman.

Wm. T. Morgan, Acting Boatswain.

A. Lloyd, Captain of Fo-Castle.

W. Rhode, Quartermaster.

Hans Schuman, Quartermaster.

Frank McShane, Quartermaster.

Fred Bruch, Bo-Swain's Mate.

Otto Polte, Captain of Main-Top.

Grank Berk, Quartermaster.

Jacob. K Johansen, Captain of Fore-Top.

Frank Helms [sometimes called Melms], Seaman.

T. Bush, Blacksmith's Helper and Seaman.

Julius Huebner, Seaman.

Otto Petersen, Seaman.

Owen McCarty, First Class Fireman.

Wm. H. Deming, First Class Fireman.

Edward O'Leary, First Class Fireman.

Robert Morelli, Ward Room Cook.

Wm. Grace, Ship's Cook.

Domnick Rooker [sometimes called Becker or Booker] Ward Room Steward (Colored)

"Peter," Dog Driver, came on board at Peterpaulacki [Petropaulovsk], hired to feed and drive dogs and was sent to his home the next year from a place in Russia.

All officers and the Crew, except Master Chas. R. Putnam, returned to the United States. At the time of this writing [date unknown], those who are dead are:

Master, Howard Scott Waring

Ensign, Henry Jackson Hunt

Machinist, Scoby Willard Morrison

Seaman, William Grace

Seaman, Theodore London

Fireman, Edward O'Leary

2. Preparation

The following account of the trip is taken from my log:

Monday, May 30, 1881 Steamship "Rodgers" turned over to Captain Robert M. Berry by the Commodore of Mare Island Navy Yard, by order of the Secretary of the United States Navy.

Captain Berry at once assumed command and sent an Order to the Captain of United States S. "Independence" to send the crew of selected men for the U.S.S. "Rodgers" to report on board for active duty. All officers and crew reported, were assigned to their respective Quarters, and at once commenced to stow away cargo. With the other Machinists we received orders to examine the Engine, boiler, Pumps, etc. and get everything in order to have steam up and turn over Engine tomorrow. My part of the work required me to go to the Navy Yard Machine shop, which I found to be a well equipped place employing a large number of men repairing Government vessels.

We had our first experience with our ship's cook during the day, and at night felt like hunting up a cheap restaurant as an improvement. I had to remind my room mates this cooking was part of the hard service we shipped for, but this day passed very quickly and all hands quit about 6 P.M., when we retired to Quarters.

Our vessel was moored to the wharf, and after supper we went to the Yard, having secured permission from the Officer of the Deck. In the room assigned to our mess were five bunks and a table, and we drew lots to see how we were to be located. I had the upper bunk. Besides machinists, the Acting Ship's carpenter and ships Yeoman had places in the room. We commenced to get acquainted with each other and with the room. We played cards, read and turned in for the night.

June 1st All day the crew were busy taking in stores, clothing, and coal. The report circulated that, as soon as we had aboard all supplies, we should start our trip.

June 2nd Received authority to-day from the Officer of the deck to have our living room fitted up and painted; had some lockers put in and the room painted; at night swung a hammock and stayed in forecastle.

June 3rd We are still taking in stores; it is astonishing the amount of stores that can be placed in a vessel. The men are getting acquainted with each other and their duties. We have some pretty rough sailors. They are already laying in a supply of trading goods, such as beads, needles, knives, cloth, etc. and as some of them have been north before, expect to get some furs and ivory in trade.

June 4th Our department stores arrived to-day. All supplies for the engineer's department were put away in the engineer's store-room. In the afternoon all hands were called on deck and had rubber boots given them—two pair to each man. We were advised to take large ones so as to be able to wear two pair of socks in them.

June 5th The cases of government clothing arrived to-day. All hands called up. We received one heavy overcoat, two pairs of pants, two pairs of drawers and two shirts. We were again given the afternoon off, as word was passed that to-morrow we would start.

June 6th At 7 A.M. orders were given to start fires. We had steam up at 8 A.M. and pulled away from the wharf and tied up to the buoy. Officers and crew all aboard. At 10 A.M. the tug "Nellie," having aboard ladies and gentlemen from the navy yard to see us off, accompanied us to San Francisco. The men on the U.S.S. "Independence" cheered as we sailed by and must have been very much surprised to hear the crew of the "Rodgers" singing a "Shantee" as it is not allowed by the U.S. navy officers, but everything goes to-day, even the tide is with us. After starting main shaft, box heated and we stopped about ten minutes to cool it off, then started again. I had charge of the engine room.

June 7th After arriving in San Francisco Bay had main bearing examined and found the babbit had melted; it took all forenoon to put it in order. As we were to receive more provisions and final orders before sailing, all men who could be spared were given shore leave. At night it was reported that Wm. J. Roach, able seaman, had deserted during the day; as the boat was leaving the ship to bring from shore the men off on liberty, Wm. Smith also deserted, but all understood that now is the time to quit if the prospect has lost attraction.

June 8th All day we have had visitors who were shown around. They seemed pleased with the ship and outfit and left for shore before dark. We received books and papers from some friends of the officers to-day. When the boat went to the wharf with the men allowed liberty for twelve hours, Wm. Smith a fireman told the crew that San Francisco was good enough for him; he then deserted. This is the third man to leave since we anchored in the bay.

June 9th All day we had visitors, many ladies among them. The Pemican food was examined and they tried to eat some of it, picked out the raisins, said it was lovely and hoped we would enjoy it.

June 10th To-day an organ, some musical Instruments and books were received on board for the use of the men. Stores and provisions were also received, and a car-load of provisions sent from the East was rejected as unfit food by our officers. Morrison and I went in and bought a lathe and some small tools, and also Remington 16-shot rifles with a re-loading outfit. We bring needles, beads, and articles to trade, as we hear from the whalemen, who go up there, that furs can be obtained from trade stuff.

June 11th Had liberty again all day. Rode on a cable car; went to the power house to seek the machinery work. With others of the crew visited Chinatown and think it a place that is of no use to San Francisco. Met Mr. W. H. Milliken, Builder of Cable roads. I started to serve my apprenticeship with him in Boston during the war. His machine shop was burned out, and he came to California and has been here since that time. Had dinner at his home, and in the evening we went to the California Theatre, then to the Occidental Hotel. Tired enough for one day.

June 12th Met Mr. Milliken early in the day, and he showed me all points of interest in San Francisco. He also introduced me to Railroad officials and newspaper men. Dined at his home. He was much interested on account of the Gamgee Zero motor that I had described to him. I worked on one in the Washington navy yard. I called at the San Francisco Chronicle office and made arrangements with the manager to act as correspondent during the trip of the "Rodgers." They furnished me with paper, pens, etc., and gave me an order to used telegraph if necessary and have all messages charged to them. I explained I had never tried this kind of work but agreed to do so if anything worth recording happened.

On June 12 the *Jeannette* was locked in a death-grip by moving pack northwest of a new landfall given the name Henrietta Island in 77° north, 157° east. "The ice commenced to pack together, bringing a tremendous strain on the ship, heeling her over to starboard and forcing the deck spans open. This continued during the day at intervals until evening, when it was evident that the ship could not much longer hold together. The boats were lowered on the ice, and provisions, arms, tents, alcohol, sledges, and all necessary equipment for a retreat securely placed on the floe. . . . On the morning of the 13th of June, about 4 o'clock, the ice opened and the ship went down, with colors flying at the masthead. —Our Lost Explorers; the Narrative of the *Jeannette* Arctic Expedition—

June 13th Reported on board at noon and went on duty in Engine room. We kept up steam and expected to get away at any time. I was called at 9 P.M. and sent on shore with a rush message for Captain Berry. He was at the Palace Hotel. I waited for and returned to ship with his answer to the officers. While I was ashore Ensign Hunt came on board with three men to take the place of the deserters. He got them from the U.S.S. "Pensacola" then in the bay. It looks as if we were to get away on our trip now. Only awaiting final orders.

June 14th The crew have had a few who would not go any further than this port; now one of the officers falls out; and it is reported that as soon as another will volunteer that a change will be made and we will start North. Master Halsey had been drinking very hard ever since we came to San Francisco, and to-day came in our cabin for liquor that Hodgson our yeoman was to get him while ashore. He had delirium tremens and was carried to his cabin. Dr. Castillo attended to him, and later in the day he was sent to Mare Island Hospital by orders of Dr. Jones. He was accompanied by Dr. Castillo.

June 15th This morning orders were received to sail, but had to wait for the officer who is to take Master Halsey's place.

3. Departure

June 16th Final orders to sail were received at 3 P.M. to-day and word passed to get ready. Fires were started at 1 P.M. Morrison had first watch from 12 to 4; Cahill from 4 to 8; Gardner from 8 to 12. All life was getting ready. Flowers were sent to the officers with best wishes of their friends. Tobacco, pipes and small stores issued to the crew. The carpenter charged all the fire extinguishers and placed them within easy reach. Mail sent ashore, and at 2.30 the Pilot reported to take us over the bar. Master Chas. F. Putnam reported on board to take the place of Mr. Halsey. at 3. P.M. sharp commenced heaving up anchor. Several vessels, the "Sausalito," "Hartley," "Gov. Irwin," and "Holyoke," with friends and music accompanied us as far as Fort Point, and flags were dipped and whistles blown as we sailed by, and hundreds of people lined the wharves, cheering us as we sailed by. After we got outside the pilot left us at 7.30, taking the mail. It began to be very rough weather and the vessel was loaded down at the bow. The seas were heavy and a stiff wind was blowing all night, which made it hard to handle the ship. Orders were passed to haul fires about 11 P.M., as we were to use sail until we reached first stopping which, we understand, is to be at Petropaulovski in Russia, where we are to get dogs, a driver and some skin clothing.

June 17th Rough weather all day; many of the officers and crew are sick during the night. Several seas were shipped; as the ship is down by the bow the water got into the forecastle, wetting the beds and clothes. Dominick, the ward-room steward is very sick and asked a favor of the Captain to "Just put me shore for the Lord's sake,"—the captain said he would think it over. Carpenter sick; Dr. Castillo sick. I stood regular watch.

June 18th Rough weather until noon. A number of the men are very sick, including DeTracey, Morelli, and Booker. The sea running high dashed in over the engine-room grating, rusting engine and shaft. The rolling of the ship has shook up the drinking water until it tastes very badly. All the crew draw rubber boots and so'wester hats; coats and pants are issued to all hands.

June 19th Nice weather to-day and all enjoy it after so rough a time. We get out our clothes and bedding to dry. DeTracey is now the only sick man on the list. All sails set and we are moving along with light winds. All vegetables are brought on deck and assorted.

June 20th Very calm this morning. Wind is dying out. At noon orders received to start fires. We take the regular watch; we are quite a ways from shore, but the gulls follow us. I caught a fine specimen to-day with a fish line, and Drs. Jones and Castillo dissected and prepared it for setting up. We expect to have all kinds of curios when we return. This is a good one for a start; it measures over six feet from end of wings. Carpenter DeTracey is still very sick. I think going to sea isn't his strong point.

June 21st Very calm this morning. We have the engine running, not at high speed. Blankets and bed-clothes are issued. Quite an accident happened to Grace, the ship's cook who went into the forehold for water and slipped, falling and breaking a rib, so for a few days everyone does his own cooking or go without.

June 22nd Steamed along through smooth sea all day. Have not seen any vessels since leaving shore. We know now our first stop will be at Petropaulovski in Russia, where we take on dogs and drivers and winter clothing. Our cook is in bad shape; his fall relieves him from duty. A breeze comes up at noon, light swell on sea. Tobacco stores and underclothes issued.

June 23rd Stopped steaming 6.45 A.M. Quite a breeze blowing and we get along with sail. English Barque passed astern of us at 10.30, signals given and answered. Wind gets heavier. Tacked ship at 2 P.M. Carpenter and cook on sick list.

June 24th Again boatswain's whistle calls, and we find that to-day rubber hats, coats, and pants are to be issued to all hands. Weather has moderated, wind lighter, and we are sailing right along. Carpenter and cook sick.

June 25th Relieved from engine-room duty to-day. Overhauled trunk; put away spare clothing; tried a new trick to-day washing dirty clothes; that is something every man on board ship has to do; it is alright after you get started. We brought a lot of "Moody" and "Sanky" Hymn Books and had some singing this evening. I am not much of a warbler and so read "Swedenborg's" Works and "Owen Meredith's"

Poems. Weather is getting rough again. We are making seven knots under sail. Tobacco and small stores issued to-day. I got two plugs, they will do for trading if we get ashore.

June 26th We get very rough weather now, quite a wind and high sea. Spray and water flies all over the ship; it is grand to look at a big green sea just as it comes aboard and dashes all over everything. The cook reports that he can take his place if a man is sent to help him. All hands are glad to have him back, as we need hot coffee anyway in this kind of weather; half-cooked grub has been issued for a few days. I know how to cook so it don't bother me. Plenty of stuff to eat on this ship.

June 27th Rough weather still continues. It is great to see the sailors dodging the waves and spray that comes aboard. We saw lots of black fish to-day, they came very near and were quite plentiful. At night we saw a large comet in the sky—it was a grand sight. Our carpenter is still sick; he says he is too weak to get on his legs. The deck has been wet ever since we started.

June 28th Very rough and stormy all day. A big sea came on board and got in the forecastle and done lots of damage to the sailor's bunks and clothing. I overhauled the hoisting engine to-day; put it in order for work; had to fix bearing. Carpenter is getting to be a nuisance in our room; there are five us in a room 7 x 10, and he should be taken to [sick] bay.

June 29th Orders to get steam up again, so I went on duty. The Carpenter's mate Quirk is quartered with us to take care of the carpenter, and also on account of everything being wet in the forecastle.

June 30th Steamed all day, light wind. All hands got out clothes to dry. It is pleasant to be on deck in this kind of weather.

July 1st Sea quite rough again. We steamed through it all day. Ship rolled and tossed until all the comforts of a home were missing. The carpenter is sorry he left Vallejo and the bosom of his family.

July 2nd Sea going down some. We are yet under steam and a light wind is blowing. Sail set. The Doctor ordered the Carpenter to come on deck and make his miserable life happier; with the assistance of the mate, he is set up outside while his bunk and clothes are put alright.

July 3rd Steam and sail set all day. Making good headway. When we left San Francisco Bay, there was a half grown pig on board, a present from some of the ladies to the officers. The ship's cook gets orders from the executor to murder said pig between the hours of 7 A.M. and 10. Order duly executed, and Denis is no more, but goes to grace the table of the ward-room mess. We live well, plenty canned roast beef.

July 4th Came on deck at 4 A.M., saw the sun rise, got some coffee and turned in until breakfast. It was very quiet to-day. No celebration except singing in the evening. Carpenter is getting better; has stopped growling.

July 5th We sailed with stiff breeze all day. Vessel on her course. Find time to read, also do odd work in engine room.

July 6th Ship on her course and to-day started to use engine again; after running awhile, bearing got hot during Gardner's watch. He is young and never had to do with marine engines, so things got the start of him—shut down for about two hours—started again at 6 P.M.

July 7th Engine working alright again to-day and we stand regular watch. Storm coming.

July 8th Very stormy all day; all hands called to wear ship; rough sea, and we run before the wind from 11 A.M. Engine run all day and we shipped a big sea; it came into our room and floated sea chest and loose bedding all around washed up to DeTracey's bunk. It began to clear up toward evening. Our poor carpenter thinks he will never get well.

July 10th Early this A.M. sighted land, one of the Fox Islands called Ouninac, and we run in sight of land all day. Now we begin to get long days, day-light at 3 A.M. lasts until 9.15 A.M.

July 11th Stopped engine, took up lost motion in boxes and crank, at 11 A.M. trimmed fires. Land is yet in sight. We are going through the Pass. While off duty I fished over side of ship. We begin to see fur seal; they come very near our vessel.

July 12th Steamed along all day with land in sight. We get stores such as flour and things we cook. Plenty is issued, and pork and beans are wasted.

[*Jeannette*] "About the 12th of July we saw a 'whale back' that looked very much like a snow-covered island. . . . The captain then shaped the course [of the shipwrecked sailors now towing their sledges over the sea ice] toward the point where land was thought to have been seen. . . . About July

20th we worked nearly twelve hours in advancing 1,000 yards over small pieces of ice constantly shifting. We could not float the boats." —<u>Our Lost Explorers; the Narrative of the *Jeannette* Arctic Expedition</u> (Chapter XVII) —

July 13th Steamed all day. We stand regular four hour watches. Everything works smooth. We lost sight of land, and foggy weather, with big, soft mosquitos, has got around.

July 14th Rainy and cloudy all day. We use sail and steam. Land in sight again; so are among lots of small islands.

July 15th Pleasant weather to-day. Land in sight. The carpenter is yet on sick list.

July 16th Pleasant weather. We have lost sight of land. Again Doctor called up all hands for examination and ordered lime juice to be issued. This helps to keep off scurvy. All our vegetables are used up. Sailors do hate to drink lime juice.

July 17th Steam all day; head wind and ship rolled until I must say I am tired tonight. No chance to read, as a light in our room slides all over the table. Carpenter is quite sick; he don't eat or try to get about.

July 18th Steam all day. Rainy and squally weather all day. Lots of ducks in sight. I do my on cooking on biscuit and coffee when I can get a chance.

July 19th Stopped engine at noon. expected to see land. Hove to until 3.45, then went ahead full speed. Outside port are three tall, rocky shafts, spoken of on our chart. Arrived in Port Petropaulovski at 7 P.M. As we entered port, boat from the steamer "Alexander" came to meet us and pilot us in to an anchorage. Then engineer Thos. Bulger came on board with some of the officers and men of the Alaska Fur Co. Steamer "Alexander"; then the Port Master and his squad came on board with physician to see if we were healthy. When I came on deck upon looking around, saw a Russian Man-o-war in port. Her name is the "Straylock."

[*Jeannette*] "Captain DeLivrou [of the *Strelok*] informed Lieutenant Berry that he had been directed to assist the searchers for the *Jeannette* in every way in his power; and during the stay of the *Rodgers* the Russians extended to her officers the most cordial hospitality. At this place a native was hired as a dog-driver, and forty-seven dogs were taken on board, whose howls for many hours afterward were something to be remembered by all who heard them." —<u>Our Lost Explorers; the Narrative of the *Jeannette* Arctic Expedition</u>—

July 20th At anchor, and visiting is the order of the day. Russian officers come on board from the "Straylok"—They are very fond of good wine and are a jolly set.

Officers of the "Rodgers" returned calls in the evening. Many visitors came on board during the day and quite a lot of trading is done by the crew in our department. We had to work on engine all day; find that our boiler is going to give us trouble; we use a jet condenser, one of the hardest kind to watch and keep in use.

July 21st Party start up coast this morning in charge of Mast Putnam to get dogs and a dog driver. Morgan is in charge of the grub and trade articles. The Russian officers kindly sent one of their men with the outfit, to guide and interpret. Expect to be back soon. It is very pleasant here. Fish are very plentiful. I have been on shore; it is a very old and odd-looking place. Many from shore have visited us and have learned of our search and know we are to get some of our stores in that place.

July 22nd This afternoon, the party that went in search of dogs returned, bringing twenty-two half starved, wolfish looking dogs, and are to select a driver from among the many application. While up the river, the boat up-set and Petersen and Morgan were thrown into the water, also stores and clothing, but they report that all was righted in about an hour, and the rest of the trip made in safety.

I got off duty and went ashore toward evening. I think the place has about five hundred to eight hundred inhabitants. There does not seem to be any business of any kind; all stores have license to trade in certain article; only one place handles cloth, another matches, another liquor; all pay a certain amount for this privilege and no other store handles the article. We found a banker who took our American gold and gave us paper and big copper money for change, charging a good price for the exchange.

I find sentinels of the Russian Army on guard at different parts of the city. On inquiry, find that during the Crimean War this was a place of great importance to Russian. For a few Kopecs, a guide who can talk English, shows us all we want to see for this trip, and asks more questions than we can answer. On the beach boats come in with salmon. I find the Bay just alive with them; they are caught in large nets and a boat is loaded with at least a ton in one haul I see fish drying everywhere; they are split and the backbone removed. Women do this work. Flies seem to cover the fish as soon as it is spread out.

We visited several houses and were welcomed, the guide introducing us. children seem afraid of strangers; all get behind their parents and take a peep at us. The young people have a happy look; are poorly dressed; all seem to be on the grab for any and everything in sight. I visited the Church in the evening. It is Russian-Greek; the priest wears a stove-pipe hat without a rim. He is a married man with a family he acknowledges. He spoke to us through an interpreter; after the service of singing; also saw him baptize a baby. During the service he chants in a voice something between a squeal and a whine, and a man in the choir sings the responses in quite a good tenor voice. The service is quite a long one. Afterwards I rowed out to the ship.

July 23rd Another lot of dogs came to-day and are taken to the ship; there is a great deal of whining and kiyi-ing. There was, also, a lot of fur clothing bought to be issued to the Officers and crew. We finished repair work on engine and boiler. The trip to this point shows our boiler not in the best condition.

I got ashore early to-day, and, with others, took a good look around. among other things, visited the Earth Works for defense, where a lot of small smooth bore cannon were mounted on rotted wooden wheels, and soldiers had old flint lock guns almost worn through from cleaning the barrels. Met a man who says he was captured from the English many years ago. He said his name was Harper, and that he was not allowed to send any word to where his home was; he had quite a time to make us understand him, as he had almost forgotten the English language. He wanted to send word to some one in England, he didn't know just where. He had a grown family and grand children. He said he had lived, and expected to die, poor and away from his people.

We had with us a Remington 16-shot rifle; it was loaded to shoot and we asked permission from the officer-in-charge for the day, who called several other officers to see us shoot; and if ever there was a surprise party, it was in this place when we fired 16 shots at gulls and pelicans without re-loading. The soldier on guard at this point had a gun that loaded with a ram rod and had a flint lock and place near the end of the barrel for powder to catch the spark.

We afterwards went on board the Russian Man-o-war "Straylok" and are invited to attend a dance to-night on shore in the only large room in the place, at the house of the governor, as they call him.

I have to go on duty at 5 P.M. to start fires, but most of the officers go to the dance. I hear they were having a very warm time and, as our chief comes aboard with a sprained ankle and some of the officers and crew are sprung otherways, I gather the following report of the dance:

After a few sets had been danced and health drunk, the health of the Emperor of all the Russians was the toast; one of our officers asked who is the Emperor now since the assassinations of the last one. It was a great surprise to them, at this point of Russia, to learn that their Emperor had been assassinated, as the vessel that brought this news came in the next day; but when they did find it out the dance was ended and the bells tolled, and next day all flags were half-mast and the news told to the inquiring people. The telegraph does not reach here, and Russian officials do not tell the people too much as it might give them a headache. We had papers aboard our ship and read accounts of the assassination of the Emperor, and they were sent on board the Russian Man-o-war "Straylock."

We are ready to sail again. The crew have done lots of trading and swapped clothes, tobacco, needles, etc., for fur clothing. We bought a lot of salmon for our men, had it cleaned and packed expressly for them, and insisted on it being clean, no flies.

July 24th After starting fires found plug had blown out; had to haul fires again and fix up. The English mail steamer that comes here twice a year, came in early, with news confirming assassination of the Emperor. We sent all mail to her and understand it will go by way of Victoria, British Columbia. We are ready and start to sea at 5.30 P.M. for St. Michaels. Steamed through smooth sea all the rest of the day. At night dogs howled and fought; one had his head in a square lard tin; he was licking the grease and it slipped in too far and he almost went crazy before he could be caught and the tin taken off. We take a driver, named Peter, who has charge of the dogs. Their feed is fish and water, they are housed on the lumber forward, and if they keep up this racket some of them will be missing before we get to St. Michaels.

July 25th We are steaming through smooth water, but slowly on account of the way the ship is down by the head.

July 26th To-day, to help relieve the ship, the two heavy anchor chains, weighing several tons, were passed along the deck by the crew to amid ship; this was a help and it took all hands. Smooth water, no sail or land in sight.

July 27th Pleasant weather, smooth sea. Going to sea is something new for the dogs, so they howl all night just to let us know they are on board. The decks are wet and it is risky to get around.

July 28th We steamed all day, smooth sea. After doctor examined crew to-day, he ordered lime juice served out and insisted on all hands taking it to ward off scurvy. The sailors just don't have any use for it.

July 29th Stiff breeze sprung up. We still use steam regular watches. The lime juice made some of the men sick.

July 30th Small stuff issued to-day, tobacco, pipes, threads, etc. Stiff breeze on port quarter.

[U.S.S. Corwin] We left Herald Island this morning (July 31, 1881) at three o'clock, after landing upon it and exploring it pretty thoroughly from end to

end.

After so many futile efforts had been made last year to reach this little ice-bound island, everybody seemed wildly eager to run ashore and climb to the summit of its sheer granite cliffs. At first a party of eight jumped from the bowsprit chains and ran across the narrow belt of margin ice and madly began to climb up an excessively steep gully, which came to an end in an inaccessible slope a few hundred feet above the water. The jagged nature of its steep sides made climbing possible, and from the sea-level the top of this ravine appeared to these ambitious but inexperienced mountain-climbers to be the top of the island. After several narrow escapes from falling rocks they succeeded in gaining the top of the ravine, when they discovered that the ascent was hardly begun. Above them was a plain surface of nearly a thousand feet in height, and so steep that the loose, disintegrating rock with which it was covered gave way on the slightest touch and came thundering to the bottom.

Kellett, who discovered this island in 1849, and landed on it under unfavorable circumstances, described it as "an inaccessible rock.". . . .This little island, standing as it does alone out in the Polar Sea, is a fine glacial monument.. . .We looked carefully everywhere for traces of the crew of the Jeannette along the shore, as well as on the prominent headlands and cliffs about the summit, without discovering the faintest sign of their ever having touched the island. —The Cruise of the Corwin (Chapter XIII)—

July 31st Pleasant weather all day. Bad leaks begin to show in the Boilers.

Aug. 1st Weather changes to drizzling rain and fog.

Aug. 2nd Fog and rain all day.

Aug. 3rd Sight land, and slowed down to enter harbor at daylight.

[*Jeannette*] "The next morning," wrote the *Herald* correspondent [Col W. H Gilder on board the *Rodgers*], "we got under way and steamed slowly on our course, in a dismal rain and fog. The lead was kept going constantly, the quartermaster calling in a dreary, monotonous voice the depth of water found at each cast of the lead. At eleven o'clock the fog lifted a little, and we could see the small settlement of St. Michael's about seven miles distant, and shortly afterward dropped anchor beyond the point of land that forms a shelter for the harbor, a few antiquated iron guns bellowing forth a salute. The fort of St. Michael's, as it is called, is an enclosure of dwellings and warehouses, the interstices filled with a high wooden fence, that was originally erected as a protection against the assaults of hostile Indians. The fence of the present day is, however, maintained rather as a shelter against the wind than to guard against savages." —Our Lost Explorers; the Narrative of the *Jeannette* Arctic Expedition (Chapter IV)—

Aug. 4th This is St. Michaels, a government station. A boat from shore showed us to good anchorage, and visitor come to the ship.

[*Jeannette*] "We left Bennett Island about August 4th. We were then fifty-three days out from the place where the *Jeannette* had sunk. We were fortunate enough in being able to launch our boats and make progress between the floes. But we still had to keep our sleds for a short time longer. . . . For the next eighteen days we were working between floe-pieces, and sometimes making as much as ten miles a day on our course to the southwest." —Our Lost Explorers; the Narrative of the *Jeannette* Arctic Expedition (Chapter XVIII)—

Aug. 5th We called in here for a load of coal sent up here for us, and to-day commenced loading it. A large launch, owned by people on shore, towed the rafts, as fast as they were loaded, to the ship. We let steam down and did some repairing of the boiler. It is a poor affair.

Aug. 6th Too stormy to run the launch to and from the ship, so the crew went in and sacked coal ready to be taken aboard ship when the weather allows. We are kept busy on boiler and engine.

Aug. 7th Worked all day on coal and in engine-room. The Exquimaux are on board all day trading furs and walrus tusks. They have holes punched in their cheeks and squirt water like a syringe. Had a row with Rhode to-day when he dumped the coal into the bunker; he piled the sacks in front of our quarters, so we could not get in for dinner. I asked him to move them. He wouldn't, then I spoke to the Officer of the deck and he said he would rather not interfere, as he was short-handed, but agreed to get out of the way for fifteen minutes and let us settle it. I went for Mr. Rhode; after fighting on deck awhile we both went into the coal hole; at the end of the fifteen minutes we both were used up and willing to quite for the day. During the fight in the coal bunker, a big piece fell on Fireman O'Leary and he was found unconscious later on.

Aug. 8th Work on boiler to-day and at night went on shore. A day means something now. Sun rises about 3 A.M. and sets at 10 P.M. Had liberty and got out the whale boat and had a sail, just to try my hand.

Aug. 9th Went ashore for oil and came back all tired out. Orders to start fires and get up steam. We loaded quite heavy, and ship swung around toward the beach and grounded, so we sail on the next tide.

Aug. 10th Went on shore early to-day, hunted and got lots of birds, and as the last load of coal was going out went on board. I bought a salmon from a native fore a few needles. Getting ready for sea all day; sent mail ashore.

Aug. 11th Started for Plover Bay, and at 8.30 we went up on a big rock and, as the tide was running out, could not get off; the ship had to be lightened and the wood and coal, that the men had to wade up in their waists for in the cold water, was thrown overboard and some put on a lighter. The ship rested at an angle of 30 degrees and anchors were put out, ready to pull off with the donkey capstan when the tide was high; we waited and the wind came up sot that with a hard pull and the sails set back, we floated off; the vessel made no water in the well, the extra sheathing did good service this time—we got away as fast as steam could take us.

Aug. 12th At 8 A.M. some of the coal is sacks that had been put on the lighter was again taken on board. We start for Plover Bay.

Aug. 13th At sea, all sails set, land in sight and steaming along.

Aug. 14th Land in sight all day. Steam up all day.

Aug. 15th Quite rough and have trouble trying to enter Plover Bay. Our yeoman, Joe Hodgson, who claimed to know the entrance here, as he has been here on a whaler, also claims to have wintered in this vicinity, was called up but could give no information about headlands. We put to sea again.

Aug. 16th This has been one of the rainy days. Land in sight all day. Foggy weather. Just about 9 P.M. it cleared up, and we went and run in and anchored in Plover Bay. Natives came on board and many of the crew went on shore.

One of the reasons we called in here was to see John Cornelius, a native that the whaling captains had taken and educated, when a boy, to read, write, speak some English and drink whiskey. He came on board, and after a visit to the officers, strolled on deck. Mr. Hodgson had charge of the stores and managed to get about a pint of alcohol used for preserving specimens, which he presented to Mr. Cornelius. Half an hour afterwards he was sent ashore drunk as a native ever was. We get no news of the parties we were in search of from Cornelius, so get ready for sea.

Aug. 17th Lay at anchor all day, and at 7.30 P.M. get up steam and start for St. Lawrence Bay. Arrived outside about midnight.

> *[Corwin]* "The *Corwin* made a very short stay at Wrangell Land (August 17, 1881), partly because of the condition of the ice, which threatened to shut us in; and partly because it seemed improbable that a prolonged search in the region about our landing-point could in any way advance the main objects of the expedition. . . . a party of officers, after erecting a cairn, depositing records in it, and setting the flag on the edge of the bluff fronting the ocean, went northeastward along the brow of the shore-bluff to a prominent headland a distance of three or four miles, searching carefully for traces of the *Jeannette* explorers, and of any native inhabitants that might chance to be in the country; then all were hurriedly recalled, and we forced our way back through ten miles of heavy drifting ice to open water."
> —The Cruise of the *Corwin* (Chapter XV)—

Aug. 18th Spread fires at 6 A.M. and run into the Bay. Here we found a Russian Man-o-War in port at anchor. Officers called on board and we visited their ship, also went on shore. Traded with natives calico, tobacco and needles for fur clothes.

> [U. S. Navy] "The *Rodgers* arrived at Saint Lawrence Bay August 18. From the Russian authorities and the officers of the Russian vessels stationed or cruising in the arctic regions, Lieutenant Berry has received every facility and all the information which they were able to afford in furtherance of the object he has in view." —Annual Report of the Secretary of the Navy, November 28, 1881—

Aug. 19th This was a busy day. Officers of the ship were busy testing compasses. Our ship was turned a complete circle [i.e. "swing ship"] while the "Straylok" was at anchor, and officers from both ships called off the readings of both compasses to make sure of variation.

Lots of natives on shore watched with great interest this part of our work, afterwards telling us they thought it some tribute the Russians demanded of us. Lots of trading done here all day and had about all the villages on board. I had a chief named Kalcot visit and gave him some coffee, molasses and bread and he was very thankful.

Another day of trading and visiting; we went on shore a while. The native huts are made of walrus hide, built low and very dirty; find all natives lousy and scurvy looking.

Aug. 29th Go to sea, heavy wind. We hauled fires and run under sail until dark.

Aug. 21st Sailing along this A.M. saw a skin canoe ahead; when we came up to them they came on board, and, from signs we understood, a white man was on shore sick; so we headed for shore to land the natives as they had been out several days; were in fact lost at sea, not knowing the direction of land. Two officers and some of the crew went on shore and, after investigation, found from papers left there that the U.S. Revenue Cutter "Corwin" had called in there and left some dogs and sleds to be called for, and possibly used in the winter. The signs that they made of a sick white man, were afterwards made out to mean that one white man had slept in one of their huts when he came in with dogs and sleds. Another false alarm, so we put to sea again.

> *[Corwin]* "A notable addition was made to the national domain when Captain Calvin L. Hooper landed on Wrangell Land (The landing was made August 12, 1881), and took formal possession of it in the name of the United States. We landed near the southeast cape, at the mouth of a river, in latitude 71° 4', longitude 177° 40' 30" W. The extent of the new territory thus acquired is not definitely known, nor is likely to be for many a century, or until some considerable change has taken place in the polar climate, rendering the new land more attractive and more accessible." —The Cruise of the *Corwin* (Chapter XV)—

Aug. 22nd Got up steam and cruised along the coast all day.

4. Into the Arctic

Aug. 23rd Sailed for Herald Island, steam and sail.

Aug. 24th Arrived at Herald Island, sent boat on shore to look for traces of vessels or men. Boat returned and reported no trace of any men ever having visited the Island.

> [The *Jeannette* had passed within fifty miles of Herald Island in February 1880 and had it briefly in sight before drifting away from it for good. The *Corwin* had in fact stopped there and explored on July 31, 1881, but whatever signs she may have left of her visit were not discovered by the shore party of the *Rodgers*.]

A board was put up marked U.S.S. "Rodgers", date Aug. 24, 1881, Robt. Berry, Commander. The island is alive with birds of all kinds, geese and ducks have nests, and gulls are very numerous and act as if they were never hunted. We could hit them with our oar, they were so near to us.

> [*Oakland Tribune*] No trace of the *Jeannette* was ever found among the acres of driftwood washed up on the beaches. The *Rodgers* set off for Wrangel Island in hopes of finding there some relic, some cairn, some sign of the missing ship. Here again he was disappointed to learn that his value on board the ship was more important than his presence among the exploring parties. Captain Berry was to lead one of the parties overland, while Lieutenant Waring's would skirt the east, and Ensign Hunt's the west coast in whaleboats.

Another noticeable fact here: when we were away about ten miles we all could see two islands, and in all old English maps, two islands are laid down, but as we sail up only one is here; the mirage that plays the trick is very noticeable in this part of the world.

[*Corwin*] "Some small fragments of knowledge concerning this mysterious country have been in existence for nearly a century, mostly, however, of so vague and foggy a character as to be scarce at all available as geography, while up to the time of Captain Hooper's visit no explorer so far as known had set foot on it. —The Cruise of the *Corwin* (Chapter XV)—

Aug. 25th Reached the ice pack near Wrangel land at 4. P.M. Steamed through the ice and came to anchor in a fine bay, deep water. At 9.45 P.M. Boat was sent ashore; it is just about twilight. Lieutenant Putnam is in charge. He planted the American flag and took possession in the name of the United States. We saw a few blue foxes and lots of birds on shore. This is the season for hatching their young.

[U. S. Navy] "On the 25th of August the *Rodgers* anchored in a harbor on the southern coast of Wrangel Land, to the westward of Cape Hawaii. She remained there until September 13, during which period Wrangel Land, or rather Wrangel Island, as Lieutenant Berry found it to be, was examined by three exploring parties organized for the purpose; but no tidings of the *Jeannette* nor of the missing whaling vessels could be obtained. Interesting reports from Lieutenant Berry, with charts and sketches of Wrangel Island, will be found in the appendix to this report. The whole coast of the island, with the exception of a few miles of outlying sand spits, was examined, and Lieutenant Berry believes it impossible that any of the missing parties ever landed there." –"Arctic Expeditions - The *Jeannette*, the *Rodgers*, and the *Alliance*," from the *Annual Report of the Secretary of the Navy, November 28, 1881—*

Aug. 26th Master Waring found a more sheltered bay, and at 11 A.M. we steamed and went in anchor in four fathoms of water; it was decided to survey this place, as it is one of the ideas circulated that, from this land, it is an easy journey to the pole. Three details of men were selected to prepare for a survey of the place.

Capt. Berry, Dr. Jones, London, Melms, Becker and Petersen were to go inland and travel five days, taking with them ten day' provisions, ammunition and some instruments. Master Waring, Dr. Castillo, Bruch, Quirk, Lloyd, McKane and Johansen were to sail in an opposite direction from the Waring party, also to look for cairns or inhabitants; both crews in a good whale-boat were to sail five days, then return; provisions for sixteen days were issued, sheep skin, sleeping bags, deer skin clothing, seal skin boots, etc.

I got off duty, went on shore, shot three geese, also got some plants; all in readiness to sail in the morning; provisions, and clothing are in the boats ready for an early start. Men not selected for survey duty are to guard ship and do necessary repairs while crew were away.

[*Oakland Tribune*] Years later Cahill expressed his disappointment at having been ordered to keep at his duty on board the *Rodgers* while other seamen were sent to explore Wrangel Island. He would very much have liked to have been among those chosen to go abroad on the island looking for traces of the lost *Jeannette* explorers, or gold. But as machinist's mate, his value was much greater to the ship than it would have been on shore. Any of the sailors could draw in harness, but few could cobble, repair, or invent the daily necessities with his skill. His lot was to stay near the ship, and watch in vain as the three exploring parties set off in search of adventure. "Would wild and savage natives spring out from the uncharted, unexplored. Would the lucky men find strange animals and precious metals? What did this mysterious island conceal?"

A house for magnetic observations is to be erected on shore at once, in charge of Lieutenant Putnam, and we are to be kept hard at work and on the lookout for the return of the different details of men.

[*Corwin*] "On the morning of August 27, having taken on board a full supply of coal and water, and put the ship in as good condition as possible, we left Plover Bay and turned once more toward Wrangell Land. . . . We have not met the *Rodgers*. We learned from the natives at Plover Bay that she had left seven days before our arrival. That was August 17. We suppose she went to St. Michaels from there to coal and take on provisions, which would probably require a week. If so we may have passed the Strait ahead of her. . . . But in case she had already been at St. Michaels, then, in following out her instructions, she could trace the Siberian coast for some distance. . . .Or, if this part of the work of the expeditions had been completed before the coming of of the gate, she may be sheltering about Herald Island or at some point on the coast of Wrangell Land" —The Cruise of the *Corwin* (Chapter XIX)—

Aug. 27th Most of the day spent in getting boats ready and party on shore. At 3.30 P.M. Ensign Hunt's boat cleared away. A hearty cheer was given and an old boot thrown at them for luck. Hunt thinks he will make a big record as an explorer before he returns. Lieutenant Waring's boat gets away about the same time, and he and his men return the cheer given from the ship. Some of us went in shore to see Captain Berry and party off. Among other things he had a sled on runners, on which was loaded instruments for observations. They also carried a tent, extra fur, clothing and provisions. Every man in this outfit had a full forty lbs. of a load to carry. We went with them part of the way to assist them with the load.

The first mountain they climbed the sled was abandoned, a cairn was made of it, records placed under it, including a bottle with name of ship, officers and crew, also the object of our search [that is, the missing *Jeannette*.] We returned aboard. Master Putnam was in charge of the ship. He ordered all fires extinguished at 9 P.M.; fire hose were connected and the watches named. Weather just fine. We are to get on shore tomorrow and experience the strange sensation of being on a place where man has not dwelt for a few centuries.

[*Corwin*] "Commander DeLong, in a letter to his wife, written at sea, August 17, 1879, said that be proposed to proceed north by the way of the east coast of Wrangell Land, touching at Herald Island, where he would build a cairn and leave records; that if he reached Wrangell Land from there he would leave records on the east coast under a series of cairns twenty-five miles apart. 'If a ship comes up merely for tidings of us, let her look for them on the east side of Wrangell Land and on Herald Island. If I find that we are being carried east against our efforts to get north, I shall try to push through into the Atlantic by way of the east coast of Greenland, if we are far enough north; and if we are far south, then by way of Melville Bay and Lancaster Sound. That he did not build a cairn or leave any trace of his presence within a few miles of our landing point does not prove by any means that he did not reach Wrangell Land at all, or that cairns with records may not exist elsewhere to the northward or westward. But the point where we landed being the easternmost point of the lower portion of Wrangell Land, it would seem from his plans as well as from known conditions of the ice to be of all others the likeliest place to find traces of the expedition." —The Cruise of the *Corwin* (Chapter XV)—

Aug. 28th Early this morning party ordered on shore to put up a large tent for magnetic observations; after tent was erected, I took a shot gun and went up the sand spit where Ensign Stoney was making a survey. He was very enthusiastic about the big thing already accomplished in landing on Wrangle Land, where we were, on shore, connected to the main land about three mile up the Coast; Gardner and I went up that way, shot and cooked some Golden Plover; found Mr. Gilder shooting as we journeyed to the main land. He is a good shot and had lots of plover; I found part of a mammoth tusk; it was about six inches through and four feet, six inches long; it had been broken off, whether in a fight or later by the ice I cannot say. It was very heavy, but as one of our whale boats came up after Mr. Gilder, I put it on board and had it taken to the ship. Gardner and I walked about twelve miles, seeing something new all the time. In the shallow water were skeletons of seals on the beach was drift wood and wreckage. We went on board at 7 P.M.

Hodgson and two natives we picked up at Plover Bay went for walrus. A heavy fog came up: we could hear them shooting and DeTracey was sent out after them, as they were in a skin canoe; all came in safe, towing a big walrus. Later, a corral having been made, the dogs were taken on shore. It gets dark about 10:30, a sort of twilight; daylight at 3 A.M.

[*Oakland Tribune*] A few days after the search parties had left [departed from the ship at Wrangel Island] the ice came crashing in around the ship, filling the sea around as far as they eye could see. By morning a large clear space was visible all around. "Now where the devil did all that ice go to?" exclaimed one of the men. Some of the men agreed with the old whaler's belief that ice sinks and rises according to some yet unknown natural phenomenon, while others thought this idea to be folly.

Aug. 29th The natives started cutting up the walrus and stowing it away for dog feed. It is for this kind of work they were engaged. I understand they are to be landed near where they were shipped and given some provision, lead, axes and knives, instead of money. I notice they can eat raw walrus, cutting off small chunks and bolting their meat without chewing.

[*Oakland Tribune*] Cahill was an astute, if not a scientific, observer of human behavior, as can be seen in his many comments about the foibles and habits of those around him. Here he notes the dining preferences of the native Masinkas who accompanied the ship northward into the frozen Arctic. They fed upon the carcass of a walrus slain on Herald Island, "with knives in their hands, blood running from their mouths. At intervals they hacked off the tenderest chunks of the animal, and crammed the raw meat into their mouths." In time he came to appreciate this mode of dining, and partake of it himself.

Sign language is all they understand yet. Went in shore and watched to work of taking observations; it is very interesting. Helped Mr. Putnam to set up and adjust instruments; also had to repair some very delicate parts that were broken in the storm, on our way here. Afterwards went out for curios; in the driftwood I found a canoe head, spear, handle, boat seat; also found a number of walrus tusks. The stones on the beach and this land are all marked with a fine line of white, crossed in various directions. The body of the stone is a gray color, and already we find specimens of fine gold flakes in the crevices washed by the action of the melting snows. I have met several of the crew looking for gold prospects. It is great getting on shore after being on board ship so long. Shooting and fishing is good. We do our own cooking and there is plenty of everything.

For some time the boatswain Morgan has had a swelling on his hand; now it is a running sore, and he is in a bad state, fears he may lose his hand. Both doctors away.

Aug. 30th Stormy weather to-day. Shot a fine mess of ducks from the deck of the vessel. During the day some of the dogs we put in the corral swam out to the ship. We hoisted them aboard. Dogs up here are a tame wolf; I think they do not lap up water with their tongues as we have seen them in our country, but immerse their mouths in the water and drink like a horse. Fear is the only thing that controls them, and kind treatment they are not used to and do not understand.

I worked to-day on a deep sea sounding device that will register depth by pressure on a square inch of a piston; it works very well and saves measuring fathoms. We have donkey boiler connected to steam pipes for heating ship.

[*Oakland Tribune*] During this time of enforced idleness, Cahill was charged with fitting out the men's quarters in the whip with steam pipes fed from the boilers. Here in the frozen Arctic the men enjoyed the luxury of steam heated apartments. The rest of the men, themselves with little to occupy their time, became cross and irritable. A new fight erupted every day. The officers stood back and let the men settle their disputes in their own way.

We tried the system to-day and it works alright. I also do most of the shoe repairing for all hands. I started fixing my own shoes and had to fix others afterwards.

Schuman is sick now; Morgan's hand is worse; Pete is our cook now—he does very well. We draw chocolate and fine store and an extra supper comes alright.

Aug. 31st Worked on boiler, also put socket bolt in fire-box. Donkey boiler is now heating ship. Sleet and snow all day. Lookout has been up in the crow's next watching for the survey parties. I find the men begin growling and want to run things. There are twenty-five very good seamen on this ship, but a continual growl is a regular thing. Several fights have occurred since my row with Rhode. Our officers are very nice about this and walk away so as not to witness an encounter. I think the only way to settle things on board ship is to let the men fight it out. To-day the French steward had a row with one of the crew and drew a big butcher knife and threatened to use it. He talks of deserting if we reach a port where he can get to civilization. I made two big iron bean pots to bake pork and beans in; perhaps feeding may stop fighting. I will try it anyway for luck.

[*Corwin*] "Thus far we had not seen the ice, and, inasmuch as nineteen summer days had passed over it since our last visit [to Wrangell Island], we hoped that it might have been melted considerably and broken up by the winds, so as to admit of a way being forced through it at some point up to the land, or so near it that we might get ashore by crossing over the coast ice, dragging our light skin boat after us in case we should come to lanes of open water.

"In this, however, we were disappointed; for when three and a half hours later we came up to the edge of the pack it was found to all appearances unchanged. It still extended about twenty miles offshore; it trended as far as we could see in the same direction as was observed before, and it seemed as heavy and unbroken as ever, offering no encouragement for efforts in this direction . . . .Towards night, when we were not far from our old landing near the easternmost extremity of the land, the *Corwin* was hove to, waiting for the morning before attempting to seek a way in. But the next day, August 31, was stormy. The wind from the northeast blew hard inshore, therefore it was not considered safe to approach too near.

"When we were within twenty miles of Herald Island we hove to, waiting better weather before entering narrow lanes and bays in the pack when so heavy a sea was running. The sky was dismal all the afternoon—toward night, dull, lurid purple—and the wind was blowing a gale. . . .September 1 was a howling storm-day, through which we lay to, swashing and rolling wildly among white waves, and drifting southeastward twenty or thirty miles a day. . . .While we were still holding on, hoping the storm would subside from hour to hour, one of the rudder chains parted.

"This made Captain Hooper decide that in view of the condition of the ship, and the ice, and the weather, the risk attending further efforts this year to search the shores of Wrangell Land should not be incurred, more especially since the position and drift of the ice held out but little promise of allowing another landing to be made, or of a sufficiently near approach to enable us to add appreciably to the knowledge already acquired. Accordingly, after the rudder was mended as securely as possible, the good Corwin, excused from further ice duty, was turned away from the war and headed for the American coast at Point Hope." —The Cruise of the *Corwin* (Chapter XIX)—

Sept. 1st Bad weather all day, but for a change go duck shooting there are a great variety of them here with curious looking heads and fine plumage. It is very easy to get them. Hodgson, Morrison, Smith and Gardner go out after walrus and they got two, also shot a seal but lost it through the ice. We had parts of the walrus head for supper. Duck and goose meat suit me up to date.

Sept. 2nd Cold, with sleet and heavy wind all day. At 7 P.M. A polar bear and cub were seen in shore. A boat was lowered and pulled in, the bears saw the men coming and started up the beach, the men followed quite a ways, then all returned except DeTracey. He kept on the chase until about six miles from the ship, when the bears stopped, and he got quite near to them. He was armed with a 16-shot Winchester rifle and was out for bear. He says the first shot he fired was at the cub; it was hit in the eye and fell; the old bear licked the blood from the wound a moment, then came for DeTracey. He fired six shots before it fell dead. He returned to the ship, received a reprimand for going off alone. A party had been sent ashore to find him but failed—he had a big bear story to tell and kept us awake until late in the night, when a report of a gun from the shore signalled us for help.

[*Oakland Tribune*] During the ten days that the three search parties had been away, the skeleton crew of seventeen men had been on the constant lookout for the wayfarers' return. Captain Berry was the first to make his way back to the ship, but as the boat came in from the shore it became clear that there there were but the captain and one other man. Cahill felt a sudden surge of fear. Had the others been left behind to die in the blizzard? Left behind for the time being, yes. But they were all well.

A boat was sent in and found Captain Berry and London; they came up the spit and reported the rest of their party footsore and played out further up the spit, where they gave out. The Captain and the men came aboard.

Sept. 3rd Hodgson and a crew were sent to search for and bring in the rest of the party. After a long search he found Booker and Petersen in the snow quite used up. He could get no tidings of the doctor or Helms, so returned with his men. Then another party started, headed up by Ensign Stoney, to look up the missing. About 10 A.M. the men were seen in shore. A boat was lowered and they were taken on board, given hot coffee and put to bed. It was very cold. Morrison and I were sent ashore to find Master Stoney and party. We went about four miles and found the boat, informed the party that all the men had got aboard.

As it was very cold, I was given a quart bottle of whiskey to be used on any of the crew that needed it, so when the boat came in to the shore to get us, I told Master Stoney that I had a bottle of whiskey if it was needed. "Pass it this way," was his order, and he was quite sick from the amount he required. It was then passed around to relieve that coldness all are subject to in the Arctic.

[*Oakland Tribune*] Dominick, the cook, and Peterson had been brought on board, both of them in a bad way, and a second boat was lowered to go after the others.

When the second lot of volunteers were called for to go search for these men on shore, quite a scene happened. Schuman had been on watch all night when Captain Berry came on board; he went with Hodgson in the first boat on shore and returned with wet clothes. He went into the forecastle, was changing his clothes when the second boat was called to go in shore; as it didn't get away quick enough to suit Captain Berry, he asked why they were waiting, answer was, for Schuman. He didn't know Schuman had been on duty about 20 hours, and when word was sent that he would come up when his clothes were changed, Captain Berry said if he didn't get a quick move on him, he would make a spread eagle of him. Schuman came on board half dressed and told the Captain that he was ready at any time to do his duty, but that there were not officers enough on the ship to make a spread eagle of any of the crew. Captain said that was mutiny. Schuman replied, "We are men, not damn fools" then went on board the boat; when the boat and men returned Captain Berry was asleep but called Schuman up; when he got about, later in the day, they had a stormy talk, and it was understood Schuman was to be severely punished when we got back and, on the part of the crew, it was hinted that some of the officers wouldn't get back. Already there was a big growl all the time between officers and men.

[*Oakland Tribune*] The sailors were in an ugly mood. "Berry talks about breaking Schumann when we get back," said one of them, "but some of the officers on this ship ain't never gonna get back." Such threats, freely uttered, did indeed come near to mutiny. Cahill wanted no part of it. Dr. Jones and Melms were the next to come on board. The doctor praised the seaman for having stayed on shore with him through the night, and saving his life. Cahill himself was ordered into the boat with Sam Morrison for the next trip ashore, to bring in the last remaining members of Lieutenant Stoney's shore party, who had fallen far behind the others on that last day of their return journey. After hours of stumbling through the wind and drift, they were all safely on board by 2:30. Cahill's sympathies were with the seaman. Morning came; the gale raged on. He waited for an inconspicuous moment to confer with Captain Berry, to get a report of the shore party's findings for his own personal log. They had covered forty miles, ascended to the height of 2,400 feet in their search, but had seen no trace of the *Jeannette*.

[See Appendix #1: "Captain Berry's Trip Inland" for Berry's own account of the first exploration of the interior of Wrangel Island.]

Sept. 4th It cleared up at noon and party went on shore to get bear skins and put up flag signals. I found part of a mammoth tusk on the beach; it was about 6 inches in diameter and 4 feet long. It had been broken off long ago, but was a fine piece of solid ivory. We went to where the bears were killed by DeTracey. The men skinned both bears, and, as we started back to go on board ship, we saw some men away off, walking very slowly, and, on account of the load they carried, looked queer.

[*Oakland Tribune*] On September 4 Cahill joined a hunting party on shore, and picked up a four-foot tusk from a long-dead wooly mammoth. Far to the west a group of men could be seen slowly making their way toward the ship. From a distance it was impossible to tell if they were white men or natives, but Lieutenant Waring's party was not yet expected back. "Look to your rifles!"

Expecting some kind of people inhabited the place, every man examined his rifle to see all was right, and, about that time, we began to find out that it was part of the party sent with Master Waring, which was returning on foot overland, carrying instruments and clothing. We hurried to their assistance. Dr. Castillo was badly used up, his feet were blistered so I helped to carry him over the streams. Others took the heavy loads of clothes and instruments and we got the men to the ship. They were used up and glad to bet back after a hard tramp. The following is an account of the trip with Master Waring, sailing east around the island.

[See Appendix #2: "Mr. Waring's Trip Sailing East" for Waring's own account of the ill-fated sea-borne exploration of Wrangel Island.]

Sept. 5th I had the day's duty on ship to-day; ice run in around the sand spit, and it is cold enough to freeze with so much of it about us; there is plenty of work at all times in our department. One has to do odd jobs like clothes making, washing and mending, at all times.

I was putting soles and heels on some heavy boots when Captain Berry came along and wanted me to do the same work on his boots; now, while I don't ship as shoemaker for the outfit, I will have to do this work. I also have done locksmith's work on guns, repairing all machines used in taking observations, that were broken in a storm.

Sept. 6th Went on shore early to-day; in searching along the beach, I found a bow and club, many fine stone specimens; also got some shells and plants for Dr. Jones, who is making a collection for the Smithsonian Institute. Coming back to the ship, I found a large mammoth tusk which Dr. Jones took charge of.

[*Jeannette*] [The men of the *Jeannette*, making their way over sea ice toward the mainland of the Lena delta in Siberia, paused at Kotelnoi Island before heading south again.] "This was September 6th, I think. We stayed there about thirty six hours. Large parties were sent out hunting, as numerous deer tracks had been seen. Next morning we got under way again and worked along the shore until about noon. . . . We continued until about midnight, and then encamped on a bleak, desolate spot. Next morning, September 7th, we shaped a course for the island of Stolbovol from the south point of Kotelnoi, fifty-one miles distant to the southwest." —Our Lost Explorers; the Narrative of the *Jeannette* Arctic Expedition (Chapter XVIII) —

Sept. 7th This morning Mr. Putnam asked me to help him in his house for magnetic observations. His magnetic needle pointer was broken too badly to be fixed on the pivot again. I took the needle off, put it on wood frame and let it float in oil; the magnetized end showed the direction quite as well as when on a pivot. After Mr. Putnam was satisfied it worked to suit him, I was allowed to go hunting specimens.

[*Oakland Tribune*] When not on duty, Cahill did some exploring of his own, walking the hills and beaches in the vicinity of the *Rodgers'* anchorage. Once on shore and alone, he was overcome with the feeling of his own insignificance in the vast and empty landscape, and the endless miles of impenetrable ice sealing off any path toward the North. But at his feet, beneath the moss, he discovered something even more striking—flakes of gold, washed down to the shore by the melting snow on the barren hillsides above.

In searching around I find specimens of gold in flake form, and others have quietly located places where, at some future time, they intend to come back and get gold. We are all of one mind and that is, this place is an upheaval of the earth and has plenty of mineral that would pay to come after.

[*Oakland Tribune*] "He had discovered gold. The crevices were thick with gold that had been washed down by the melting snow. Members of the crew gathered it in cans. All resolved go go back some day and get riches." [It is worthy of note, that reports of these riches when made back home, did not seem to ignite a gold rush to Wrangel Island.]

All the stones have straight white streaks about 1/16 to 1/4 in. crossing at all angles. Some quartz rock has also been found.

While returning to the ship, I saw quite a high mound of snow and started to investigate. When about fifty yards from it, a big bear that had been resting in the crater of it raised his head and took a look at me. I had an Enfield rifle that carries a big bullet about a mile, and got ready to shoot if I had to, but I started for the ship. Can't say I liked the looks of this particular bear. He also started in the opposite direction and I was glad, as I don't think he was my bear anyway. I met some of the crew after I had gone around a point of an iceberg; they asked why I was running; I told them a big bear was in sight. They started after him and fired at and halted him, but didn't get him, but they did conclude I was no hunter, and I think so on the quiet.

[*Corwin*] " . . .we found them (polar bears) everywhere in abundance along the edge of the ice, and they appeared to be very fat and prosperous, and very much at home, as if the country had belonged to them always. They are the unrivaled master-existences of this ice-bound solitude, and Wrangell Land may well be called the Land of the White Bear" —The Cruise of the Corwin (Chapter XV)—

Sept. 8th Again had the day's duty on ship; worked all day on the boiler; it is full of patches and plugs now. A jet condenser is hard on a boiler even when a good one is used; had boiler and engine room cleaned up. Since we have been anchored here, we get all the game, young geese, ducks and plover that we can use, also lots of water fowl the Doctor has to find a name for. He prepared the skins for mounting.

Sept. 9th Had to make a sun dial to-day for Ensign Stoney; he is doing some surveying and dreaming of the girls he left behind him. If his names of places go on record, it will give an idea of some one he thought about when he tries to sing, "In the gloaming, Oh, my darling"—one place he names Cape Florence, another point, Atherton, and wants the island named Atherton. Bossing Dominick, the steward, and thinking of his best lady, keeps him busy.

Sept. 10th It started to rain, so I stayed on board and fixed up tools, mended clothes, got out heavy winter clothes, worked on log; have some letters written, if ever a chance to send them comes. We expect to get out and meet the home-bound whalers soon.

Sept. 11th Got ready for a long tramp, took shot-gun with heavy and light shot and lots of it. Shot ducks and snipe until I had plenty. Hung my game on a native spear handle that I found among the drift wood on the beach. I afterward gave this spear to Dr. Jones. Then I climbed over a hill and looked down in a valley that was alive with white geese; thousands of them were at rest on the ground. I went near enough to get a shot, loaded both barrels of the gun with heavy shot. They began to notice me and make a noise. I was near enough, so fired among them; the report from my gun made them rise in the air, and I fired again.

I don't think any man ever witnessed such a sight. I do know with two shots I killed a number, but the noise of their voices and flapping of wings, as they rise like a big white cloud, seemed to take all the air away from me, so I ran down the hill and didn't look for my geese, only as they circled around, screaming loud enough to make themselves heard for miles. Away to the right I saw a hilly part of the island where the snow hadn't fully melted from last year. I started over to see how it looked close by, and on my way came close to a blue fox, but my gun hadn't been loaded since I fired at the geese, so I had to admire him as he ran away. I found the place very rough when I got there. Saw tracks of bears and, fearing to meet one, just stopped long enough to take a good look from this high point at the surrounding country. I had to think of other places better known to me, and, thinking about home, wrote with my gun in the snow such names as Emma, Edna, and Belle, in large letters.

At 2 P.M. Started for the ship; met some of the crew and gave them my game, and spear, that I had found; then started among the drifted ice that came in around the spit. I saw a big white fish eagle, the biggest bird in this country. He flew very near to me and acted curious. He would fly down at me as if to scare me away from something, betting bolder every time he came. I was thinking how nice he would look as a specimen, and so got ready to shoot him; as he flew at me again, I fired, and he came to the ice; I dropped the gun and found him, as I thought, dead. I folded his wings, put him under one arm, caught his feet with one hand and his beautiful, gold-colored, knife-edge beak with the other, leaving the gun where it lay, and started up the beach for the ship with my prize. I hadn't gone far when I found he was not dead, only stunned and strong and ready to give me trouble; but I held on to him, not allowing him to use either beak, wings or feet until I got to the observation house, where Lieutenant Putnam ran a pointed instrument through his heard, and killed it before I let go. I gave it up for the ship's collection for the Smithsonian; when preparing it for stuffing, it was found only one shot hit it, and the skin was perfect. It was a fine addition to the bird collection. The bill, feet and eyes were like old gold; it measured seven feet from tip to tip of wings.

Sept. 12th Had the day's duty again. The ship was swung around a complete turn to test the compass; when as far north as this, the needle points about east and south, if anything; not being a navigator I only hear them calling off the points as the Ensign registers; at 6 P.M. Ensign Hunt's boat was seen returning—it got alongside about 8 P.M. The men were in good shape and were very glad to get back to the old ship. We helped them get their boat and instruments on board, then after supper sat up late to hear of their wonderful trip, as told by O'Leary.

[See Appendix #3: "Edward O'Leary's Trip Sailing West" for his account of the westward sea-borne exploration of Wrangel Island.]

Sept 13th Now all have returned to ship and we are to leave for Point Barrow. Started on our way at 9 A.M. and went in search of the boat Master Waring abandoned when his men started to return by the shore on foot.

[*Oakland Tribune*] Heavy ice inshore had forced them to abandon their boat and make their way homeward on foot. The boat was hauled far up the beach and turned over, the spot marked with a mast to be retrieved later.

When we came to the place where it could be seen in shore, the ice was packed too close to go in for it, as it would be hard to make a landing. We saw several whales in towards the shore, and, with the marine glass, could see bears in on Wrangel Island. It was getting very cold, heavy ice was drifting, and, as we sailed toward the open water, the crew fired at a seal and walrus. The seals we caught were called hair seal, and differ from the fur seal that we met as we came through the island pass.

[*Oakland Tribune*] They had seen no trace of the *Jeannette*, but had come upon a flagpole and a cairn erected by the revenue cutter *Corwin*, also searching these northern seas for the lost exploring ship. Inside the cairn was a message: "The *U. S. S. Corwin*, Captain C. L. Cooper, visited this land in search of tidings from the *U. S. Str. Jeannette*. A cask of provisions will be found on the second cliff to the northward. All well on board." Cooper had taken possession of Wrangel Island in the name of the United States.

5. The Arctic Whalers

[*Oakland Tribune*] While standing on deck that morning, Cahill heard unfamiliar voices speaking in English. There was no one around within earshot whose voice he did not already know all too well, and no one else to be seen. Could it be the ghosts of the lost explorers? Or better, their living souls come from over the ice? The forward lookout shouted, "Ship ahoy!" Through the binoculars a whaling ship—the *Coral* as it turned out—was just in view twenty miles away. So still was the Arctic air this day, that the sounds of the *Coral*'s men were audible over that great distance.

Sept. 14th Early this morning sighted an American whaler; we steamed up to her and found it was the barque "Coral"; the crew were frying out blubber. Our officers went on board and learned that some of the natives had found wreckage, that had drifted in shore, of the lost whalers "Vigilant" and "Mt. Wollaston"—they also heard that both wrecked vessels had drifted in with the ice and had drifted back to sea again, but the natives had taken some of the personal property from both vessels, which was shown to the officers of the U.S. Revenue Cutter "Corwin", which vessel sailed a few days ago for San Francisco with news and mail. The "Coral" had made a very good catch, had fourteen whales for the season's work and was soon to leave for home, so we sent all mail aboard.

[*Oakland Tribune*] The ships enjoyed a pleasant gam in this remote sea at the top of the world, exchanging greetings and mail. Captain Coon would be leaving soon for warmer climes. But not before taking a whale that rose to the surface nearby.

Several other whalers were in sight, and, while we waited for the boat that brought the mail to the "Coral" to return, we saw a crew kill and capture a large whale, as it rose about one thousand feet from us; was sighted by the lookout in a big hogshead at the mast head who gave the alarm calling "A blow! A blow!"

Several boats were dropped into the water in less time than it takes to write it and rowed toward where the whale was heading. It was feeding and throwing showers of water from the head, and then it went beneath the water again for a few moments, when it came to the surface again. One of the boats, that puled ahead and was very near, fired a bomb gun and at the same time the harpooner threw and landed a harpoon in the whale. The cartridge that is fired in a bomb gun has about enough force to penetrate four feet into the whale's body, then it explodes and it tore a hole in the side about as big as a whale boat. The whale moved a little ways off, but was mortally wounded and sank until it was dead, when it floated to the surface and was towed alongside of the vessel to be cut in and taken aboard. We learned from the whalers that the value of a whale of that size is about $5,000 to $10,000; so it is quite a prize. Whales are finding other feeding grounds and are harder to catch. Some of the whalers talk of wintering at Point Barrow, the place where we go next. By staying up here all winter, they are on hand when the ice breaks and whales have not been chased—they are frightened at the sight of a ship.

I went on board of a whaler and can say it is not just the kind of a life a man will hanker for, but it helps some young fellows to be better satisfied with things at home.

[*Oakland Tribune*] Other whalers hove into view and continued to linger in the area, pressing their luck against the advancing winter in hopes of bringing home their own fortunes in oil and bone.

Sept. 15ᵗʰ Cruised around and went near enough to talk to officers of the whalers. As the boat Master Waring left ashore is now to be abandoned, our Captain is trying to buy a whale boat from any of the whalers, but so far has not got one. The "Coral" is in close to us again. Her small boats have made fast to a bowhead whale and the crew look happy; this makes a big catch for this old hooker. Ice is in sight all around. The officers have just figured out our bearing. At present, 79° north, the air is so rarefied and everything quiet up here, that we can hear the men on a whaler more than twenty miles distant, in fact, below our horizon, driving up hoops in oil casks. Birds are very numerous when a whale is being cut in, as they get scraps; and when a skeleton is cut loose, after all blubber is cut off, thousands of gulls get a feed before it sinks out of sight.

Sept. 16ᵗʰ Early this morning came to Herald Island again. A boat was sent to look for the cairn left by the officers of the U.S.S. "Corwin." I was one of the crew; it was so rough that at this time we were unable to make a landing. This island rises abruptly from the sea and thousands of water fowl make it their home. They were so numerous and came so near that we hit some of them with an oar. It was decided to go back to the ship; after boat was taken aboard we started for Point Barrow. We notice the cold weather comes to stay, and it is particularly hard on the engineer department; when in the engine room, the thermometer registers 90°, and we go on deck to our room and it is often as low as zero, so we have to be very careful and not catch a bad cold.

[*U. S.* Navy] "The country is indebted to Lieutenant Berry and the party under his command for their energetic labors while at Wrangel Island, the results of which have satisfactorily established the character of that formation, and the probability that the *Jeannette* never touched there. . . On the 16th the *Rodgers* left Herald Island and proceeded to the northeastward as far as latitude 73° 44' north, longitude 171° 48' west, which was as far as the ice pack would permit; returned to the northeast point of Wrangel Island, and took a course in a northerly and westerly direction in the hope of finding the high land north of Wrangel Island, reported as "situated in 178° west longitude, and extending as far north as 73° north latitude, as the eye could reach," by Captain Smith, of the whale bark *New Bedford*. She crossed the 178th meridian and reached a position in latitude 73° 28' north, and longitude 179° 52' east, and then recrossed the same meridian in 73° north without sighting land, the horizon and sky being at the time clear to the northward." –"Arctic Expeditions - The *Jeannette*, the *Rodgers*, and the *Alliance*," from the *Annual Report of the Secretary of the Navy, November 28, 1881*—

Sept. 17th Steaming along all day and met quite a lot of whalers; saw Herald Island and a beautiful mirage. We have an old map that shows two islands called Herald and Plover Island, both are to be seen when we are about ten miles away, but when we sail up close, one seems to go into the other, and we sailed over the place where we saw Plover Island. The whalers seem to be doing a big business this week.

[*Jeannette*][The surviving men of the *Jeannette* make a landfall on the mainland of Siberia, in the delta of the Lena River.] "At this juncture Bartlett spoke up and said that he believed we were in the east branch of the Lena. . . .The trend of the river corresponded pretty well with the coast outlet, and if we could find an island about thirty miles ups stream it would, doubtless, prove that we were in that place. . . . So we stood up stream and were fortunate enough to make a landing at seven P.M., in what we found afterward the native Tunguses call an *orasso*, or summer hunting hut. We had been 108 hours in the boat since leaving Semenoffski Island." —Our Lost Explorers; the Narrative of the *Jeannette* Arctic Expedition (Chapter

XIX)—

Sept. 18th Steaming all day. Herald Island in sight. Quite a lot of walrus seen all day. Whaler "Progress" seen in the distance—one of her boats fastened to a large bowhead whale.

Sept. 19th Running north again; plenty of ice all around; fog and storms most of the time. Ship came to anchor, and boat sent on shore, commanded by Mr. Waring, to land and look for the cairn on Herald Island. I went in the boat; was near enough to jump on shore, but could see no way to climb the steep side of the island; passed the nests of many thousand of sea gulls and ducks; the gulls are so tame that they flew withing ten feet of us; saw new specimens of birds; had taken no shot gun so did not get any game. After sailing several miles along the coast, it was decided to return to the ship, as it was too rough to land at any place we saw. Got on board all right; boat hauled up.

I went on duty, as Gardner had stood my watch while I had been off. We then went North through the ice, reaching the heavy ice. The "Rodgers" is a good ship for butting ice. Many of the men do not like the idea of running into this pack, and so expressed themselves. On the ice we saw and fired at Polar bears, but they were too far off; none were hit. We kept on steaming, through the pack, North, until 6 P.M., when it was getting dark. Several of the men were sent out on the ice with an ice hook, and we made fast and anchored to a large cake of ice; then quite a lot of us had a run on the ice, and then turned in.

Sept. 20th At day break cast loose from ice, and began to butt around in the pack— once ran heavily into a projecting piece of field ice; it was fast getting foggy and cloudy. When it had cleared off in the afternoon, we had reached quite a lot of clear water. A large Polar bear was seen swimming toward the field ice—nearly everyone that could get hold of a rifle kept firing at him—the ship steered towards him and finally he was killed—as usual in such cases, everyone that fired killed him. He was taken on board, the scales were rigged up, and with the lead in him weighed 1,000 lbs., (2/3 bear, 1/3 bullets).

Mr. Stoney claimed the skin; it was given him, and afterwards sent home by the "Progress." Today we reached the farthest point North that any vessel on this side has gone, 73° 45'. The ice was now all around us, solid to the north—no sign of a lead could be seen. We hove to until daylight; all hand had a good sleep. The men who had been up here on the other expedition, were the most alarmed, and I think they unnecessarily create alarm in the minds of those of us who are up here for the first time. If I am here again, I prefer not to have anyone for a shipmate that knows too much about the Arctic. We find out, soon enough to satisfy us, the dangers of the search, without having Hodgson's imaginary adventures to think over.

We get very good food now. Lime juice was daily issued. None of the men were sick, but the deck was always wet.

Sept. 21st Could not proceed north on account of ice; sailed toward Herald Island; it seemed to be a favorite place of ours. When we neared land a heavy fog sat in, and we came to anchor. Here the currents were tested, and noted not running as strong or as fast as reported by Whalers. Efforts were made, as the fog lifted at times, to see Herald Island, but no use. It rained and drizzled to make things comfortable. The rigging looked as if Jack Frost had made it; very slippery on deck; and the dogs kept up a continued howl and nuisance; many of them had fits nearly every day. One jumped overboard—a case of suicide. When the fog lifted, up anchor, and we again went to Wrangel Island to get the boat abandoned by the Waring party. Stored it under it were several sleeping bags and quite a lot of deer skin clothing, that would be useful to the men when making sledge journeys. So Captain Berry was determined to get the boat and clothing if possible. Quite a lot of broken ice floating, fog and rain; at intervals when cold—snow. Men at this time, seeing so much ice, thought it time we were to get to winter quarters.

Sept. 22nd At daylight could see, through the fog and light rain, the coast of Wrangel Island. We had quite a lot of loose ice to run through to run in, and had to slow down. We came to the point where the boat could be seen; a boat was lowered, and went in, commanded by Mr. Waring. They reached the shore and got the abandoned boat and its contents safely afloat. It was found that a Polar bear, that had been seen near the place, had eaten the pork left in the boat; every thing was found in quite good condition. The ice was now fast running in shore, and it was with great difficulty that the boats were able to reach the ship, which they finally did, and they were hauled on board—had the party delayed even half an hour, neither boat could come through the ice, so fast did it drift in toward the beach; while the boat was in shore, on board ship we were firing at walrus and seal, that were here in great numbers. None killed, as usual. There have been a great lot of cartridges used up in practicing—even if a shot took effect, the animal would sink before a boat could be lowered and got away.

Sept. 23rd We were steaming near Herald Island all day quite a lot of ice seen on port side. In the afternoon a heavy snow-storm. It made it disagreeable on deck.

Sept. 24th Slowed down last night and at daybreak ran toward the Siberian Coast. Snow storm had ceased and it was quite cold.

Sept. 25th As usual, we slowed down at night. All day running along the Siberian

Coast. Lots of ice in sight, which makes it cold. Our main boiler has been overworked, and is now badly in want of repair; it leaks in several places in both fire boxes; we must soon stop to repair it, or depend on sail. The soft coal makes it a little Hell in the engine-room.

*Sept. 26*th Hauled fires to clean and repair main boiler; for several days the Captain has been on the lookout for a homeward bound whaler. He wishes to send home is report and his intentions concerning winter quarters. The boiler was found to be in a very bad condition. We started at once to repair it and found several tubes leaking badly; they had filled the back connection with salt. We could see Wrangel and Herald Islands from where we lay. Quite a lot of whale seen here, and we expect soon to meet with whalers.

*Sept. 27*th At daybreak seven sails were sighted; sure enough there were whalers in all directions. All necessary repairs done on boiler, so we at once took up steam and made for the Steamer "Belvedere," sister ship to the "Rodgers." They were fortunate to-day, having caught a large bowhead whale. One of these whales is now valued from $6,000.00 to $10,000, so it is quite a prize. They had taken fourteen whales and, with three more, would fill up a very good season. A boat was lowered, Captain Berry went on board. When he came back to the ship he brought on board a native interpreter, that was educated in New Bedford, John Cornelius. The Captain made arrangements with him—he agreed to go on sledge journeys this along the Coast. The Captain was to send for him to Plover Bay and bring him to St. Lawrence Bay, where it was decided now to winter. Mr. Gilder [the onboard correspondent to the New York *Herald*] made use of him to give him the right names of such articles as we had to trade and what we wanted of the natives. He then came to our room for supper and for a time we had a pleasant talk, finding out many facts, to us important, about the people we were to deal with during our stay in search for the missing whalers.

One of our messmates had met Cornelius before; they talked awhile and then went on deck and down to the yeoman's storeroom; here there was quite a lot of alcohol and strychnine mixed for preserving specimens, and fire for small stoves; no one except the lowest order of dirty drunkards would drink it, as it was partly poisoned, and no man would offer it to a person. But our famous Arctic truth stretcher took some and also induced Cornelius to take it; the result was that both were in a very few minutes drunk and abusing each other, and disgracing our quarters. As long as that lot of alcohol lasted our yeoman took his regular whiff at it. We put mail on board and run to Herald Island. Mr. Hunt and Stoney with a crew went in to look for cairn left by the "Corwin." After some trouble they landed and tried to get up the steep cliff, but had to take the boat; it was getting dark.

Sept 28th And Mr. Hunt thought he had been sent to examine that cairn, if it took all winter; the men in the boat had no food for eight hours—night and snow storm at hand—he could see the ship's lights and signals sent up; yet in the open boat he kept all hands until daylight, when other boats were lowered and sent out to look for him; finally the boat was seen and we steamed towards it, and picked them up —the men all hungry and cold—Captain Berry spoke quite severely to Mr. Hunt for acting as he did, endangering life and unnecessary suffering. The crew, that had been compelled to sit in the boat all night and watch the ship, every moment in danger—snow and heavy sea all around—well, they gave a sailor's blessing.

6. Shore Station on Cape Sergkaman

Sept. 29th Smooth sea. Quite pleasant to-day. Running to Cape North, where, if possible, a party is to be landed to make sledge journeys and take magnetic observations during the winter. Yesterday Signal Quartermaster Rhode told Master Charles to go to hell; to-day he was disrated and sent forward. Frank Smith rated Signal Quartermaster and Frank McShane rated Quartermaster— both cases a very good selection.

Toward night it began to blow and at mid-night was quite stormy. Yesterday Mr. Putnam and Mr. Hunt with men landed and examined a cairn of no importance to us. A large walrus was shot and brought to the ship.

Sept. 30th Heavy wind to-day. Land in sight. We could see the natives running along the shore, thinking we were to land, and we also could see the native villages. But we could find no good harbor. Sail furled and wind howling. At night we ran out from the land into deep water and hove to until daylight.

Oct. 1st The storm increases to a gale, and we hove to and rode it out. This is one of the worst days we have had; many of the men are sick. Whenever there is rough weather somehow there is no cooking done, and it seems when men need food most there is a scarcity of it; between the galley and the pantry I manage to get along at such times. Down below, the tossing of the ship works up the old bilge water and old blubber mixed, and creates quite a stink.

Four hours below, bunged up in all directions, is a hard day's work. When the ship is rolling we get tossed with great force against the sides; it is fun to see a lot of men getting out of the way of big waves and spray that comes on board. One cannot sleep, only lay awake and hang on, or brace yourself against something when it is rough.

Dr. DeTracey can sleep in his boats, in case he wants to go out and count stars. To-night water got into the forecastle, wetting all the bunks and floor. This makes it bad for the men. Water at times one foot deep on the floor. Many of the dogs have fits in this kind of weather. The lumber on deck broke loose with the heavy seas that kept washing over us. One of the dogs was killed and several were hurt. It was all a man's life was worth to be on deck; too dark to see anything. Carried away the jib; it ran up the mast head, and continued to flap and shake until it tore off.

We will remember this night until a worse one comes.

Oct. 2nd At daylight commenced to clear up the deck and secure the lumber again. Sailing towards the shore, we reached the most western point any vessel has been in this latitude. A heavy storm arose during the day and kept up at intervals during the night. We ran into deep water and hove to at night for safety.

[*U. S. Navy*] "The *Rodgers* returned to Herald Island and finished its examination, which was fruitless so far as finding any traces of the missing parties. Proceeding thence to the coast of Siberia, Lieutenant Berry examined the coast from the ship to the eastward to a point as far as Cape Serdze, and there put up a house and left a party of six, under command of Master C.F. Putnam, to remain for the winter. They were bountifully supplied with clothing, provisions for one year, dogs, sledges, &c., and will explore the coast in search of the *Jeannette*'s crew and the survivors of the *Mount Wollaston* and *Vigilant*." –"Arctic Expeditions - The *Jeannette*, the *Rodgers*, and the *Alliance*," from the *Annual Report of the Secretary of the Navy, November 28, 1881*—

Oct. 3rd Snow storm still continues. We steamed all day.

The cook treated us to a new dish to-day. All hands had complained that the coffee had a very bad taste—one of us, more inquisitive than the rest, before carrying the big coffee pot back to the galley, looked into it, and found a big, dirty, greasy swab; there was lots of cussing and the men complained to the executive officer—the cook got a lecture and he heeded it.

Oct. 4th All day we sailed in sight of land. Quite cold. We were running south; found no place to leave a party near Cape North, so are to build a house, leave party of six men with provisions for one year on the island near Sergkaman.

[*Oakland Tribune*] The *Rodgers* anchored offshore and landed the scantlings of a hut and supplies for the scientific and observation base to be established on the Siberian mainland at Eeteetlan, under the command of Lieutenant Putnam. The hut consisted of a small house with double walls and a "very leaky" roof. The curious native "Chook-Chees" crowded around day and night peering through the windows at the white men. Those assigned to the base were Putnam, Dr. Jones, Gilder, Frank Melms, Oluf Petersen, and Tatarenoof (also known as Pete), the dog-driver brought up from Petropaulovsk.

Oct. 5th Came to anchor. Captain went on shore and selected a place to put up house. At once, material was put into the boats—lumber and tools—taken on shore. The carpenters went to work building a house. Smith was added to the carpenter's force; we had lots of work all around. One boat was at work all the time bringing in stores. The native chief and all his men were always ready to help us. The chief is a big well-built man. All day long, the ship was crowded with hungry natives. They had boots, mittens, sealskin pants and other things to trade for hard tack or tobacco. I obtained a nice lot of white fox skins, well tanned and scented with musk, also white sable enough for trimming, in case they are wanted for a cloak. I have quite a lot of nice furs now to take home. I do not think we will have to pay duty on our stuff. We do not use much of our hard bread and always are ready to feed these natives, although it is against the regulations, but we may need their help in many things.

On shore I have seen them eat stinking walrus meat raw; all the scraps from our mess I give to the women and children; "Cast thy bread upon the waters" is a good motto. If it don't return, all right. All the people dress in furs; they look like the great Un-washed, one of the lost tribes. I have had a walk on shore to their huts. At one hut was a baby about seven months old, laying on deer skins. All the natives take off their clothing when they go under the deerskin curtain to the only room in the hut. They gave me some cooked walrus. It was tough.

Oct. 6th Quite rough to-day. The boat going on shore with lumber was caught in a squall, and was drifting out to sea; another boat was sent out and helped them to land. We kept up steam all the time in case the wind became stronger. Provisions were sent on shore as fast as rough weather would allow.

Many natives on board. Kanna came to our room—he brought a young seal skin to make a big cap with. He could speak a little English—we gave him hard tack and molasses—I receive two fine deer skins, heavy shirts and a cap for a number of knives and tobacco I got in San Francisco.

The men worked on the house until dark. It is sixteen feet square and the stores are to be left outside under cover of canvas and snow. Mr. Putnam is to have charge; Mr. Gilder, Dr. Jones, "Frank Melms, Petersen and Peter," seamen, are selected to remain with him—a good selection.

Oct. 7th The wind came up to a gale, we were dragging anchor so we pulled up and went into deeper water. Came to anchor again.

I got a squirrel-skin under shirt to-day for tobacco, and some sealskin stockings. I am quite well fixed now for winter. In the afternoon I went on shore and all around the little island. It looks to me as if this island were thrown up from the bottom of the sea. On the top, hundreds of feet from the shore, are the skeletons of whales, very old looking, and certainly the Indians never hauled them to the top of the hill; then buried in the rocks are the walrus that supply these people in food during the greater part of the year.

When a walrus is caught, it is taken on shore and cut up; the carcase is sewn up in the skin, all except the head; then it is left on the ground and covered with stones to keep the dogs, foxes, gulls and crows from eating it. It smells bad after the sun has shone on it awhile, but they say it is good in the winter. There are not as many caught now by these natives as formerly. Vessels come up here for walrus oil, and kill thousands of them each year, only taking the blubber, throwing the meat and skin away, which are highly valued and of great necessity to these people. Many of their villages, we hear, are short of walrus meat, and the people die of hunger. The whales are numerous, but each year keep farther from the shore, where the natives cannot reach them. One whale supplies a big village with oil and food for a long winter. So the poor natives complain of their treatment, and rightly, too, for even when whale and walrus are plenty, it is hard enough for them to catch them with their rude instruments.

The house is nearly done and provisions fast coming on shore. In the evening the Captain and Waring sent up rockets and burned blue lights. It pleased and frightened these people.

Oct. 7th Early this morning another boat and crew added to the number carrying in soft coal and provisions. Many trips to be taken; the whaleboats are splendid for sailing and landing; easy to handle either with sails or oars.

At noon, I went on shore again.. The house is nearly done, there are lots of natives lying around on the grass and sand. We got the children to dance their Hulo Hulo. It is a funny dance, all exercise of arms and legs.

Oct. 8th The dogs were taken on shore, seventeen fine ones, and seemed glad to be able to run around. As the darkness was fast coming on the house was finished— we shook hands and went out to the ship. At 8 P.M. we went to sea, the wind and storm increasing, sailed north again, to look for new land; quite cold. Boiler in very bad condition, and should be repaired—tubes are leaking.

Oct. 9th Storm still continues, and heavy sea; very cold. It is time we went to winter quarters; lots of ice in sight all around; some field ice about; put about for St. Lawrence Bay.

Oct. 10th Rough and storm weather. Boiler in very bad condition, almost impossible to keep up steam. Wind ahead making it hard sailing. At night shipped a big sea; water in the forecastle again. Very uncomfortable all around. Too rough to sleep; knees sore from bracing against top and side of bunk.

> [*Oakland Tribune*] While the ship remained anchored offloading the materiel for the observation base, a gale on October 11 threatened to sink the whole enterprise. The sailor Franz Bruch was swept from the deck by one huge wave, and swept back up on it in the backwash, before the shout of "Man overboard!" could be raised.

Oct. 11th Heavy gale and rough sea continued all day. At night all square sail taken in; jib tore away and made a big racket; heavy sea came in and set the lumber adrift; have to heave to until daylight; Then it was a sight on deck; everything piled up just as the waves had left them; the men all wet and used up; forecastle floor had over a foot of water; men get no sleep, and, as usual in stormy weather, very little food during the day; Bruch was washed overboard on a wave and washed in again; all done so quick he hadn't time to think.

Oct. 12th Quite calm after the storm; Men at work clearing up after the night's storm—lots of damage done. Dogs have fits; one taken up on the poop deck; one walked overboard in a fit. The officers tried to shoot him in the water and end his struggles, but he was not hit—I was glad to get a little sleep.

Oct. 13th Ship on her course for St. Lawrence Bay. Cloudy weather—no sun to-day. We got through the straits [Bering Strait] all right. It was very cold. As usual slowed down at night.

Oct. 14th Passed East Cape; some natives came out in a canoe with a letter to Captain Berry, from the German Professor and Doctor that are to winter up here. The letter was read and the canoe set off toward the shore, having gained nothing for all their trouble. These natives are led to think that every letter or paper given them is of great importance. One came on board with a letter given him by some American gentleman who had employed him as a guide—the letter stated he was a thief, we found out that he was even worse than his letter stated.

At night we came to anchor, to run in at daylight.

7. Preparing to Winter at St. Lawrence Bay

Oct. 15ᵗʰ Up anchor at daybreak, and run into the bay. Here we found the whaling Barque "Progress"—I went on board with others, met Captain Barker, had a long talk with him about whaling—he said he had been wrecked and had to winter up among these people; they kept him alive, and now when they come on board he always gives them hard bread and molasses. He says it was hard for a civilized man to get used to their filthy ways; that everything was washed in urine, even the spoon and dish he used to eat his walrus from, but then there was only one thing to do, grin and bear it.

He had run in here, out of the heavy gale to dry out blubber—his vessel had been cleaned up and everything was ready to start for home. Waiting only for a wind. Took mail from our ship, and when I was coming away he gave me a large bundle of papers. It was from him that I heard that the President of the United States had been shot by a crazy man, and was, at the time of the sailing of the ship, in a dangerous condition. He told us that the Whaler "Thos. Pope" had, early in the season, filled up with oil and gone to Frisco and had returned for a second trip this season with mail for us and, I suppose, late papers telling us of the condition of the President. I hope he may recover; I was in Washington at the time of his inauguration; have also seen and heard him in Congress; and went home to New Hampshire to vote for him.

A party is to go over to Plover Bay, when this "Thos. Pope" will go in, if she does not come here. We are on the watch for her, anxious for news. We brought some potatoes to the ship to try and make yeast, as the baking powder was nearly gone; Captain Barker told me he had a lot of saleratus, if I wanted it. It was afterwards brought on board; we took a lot of black skin of the whale; I ate some of it and found it quite good. The natives are very fond of it—either raw or cooked. In the evening our men visited the ship, and Mr. Stoney visited the forecastle in search of a quartermaster.

Oct. 16th In the evening, the men from the "Progress" visited the ship; one of them told me he had no tobacco; I gave him a plug, then he sent me a pair of army shoes by the boat that brought the mail.

To-day the dogs were spent on the spit near where we lay. Some of the lumber was towed in, and piled up. We also towed the "Progress" out to the head, where there was a good breeze.

The boiler worked very badly, and we made slow work of it; after leaving the "Progress" to continue here homeward journey, carrying in the last mail we can send this year, we went back to anchorage, and hauled fires; it was a very pleasant evening, not very cold. In the evening we have singing in our quarters. The natives had been on board all day, and sailed out and back with us, looking through the skylight to see the engine at work; they also climbed the rigging to show us they were not afraid.

Oct. 17th The lumber gotten on shore, the deck was for the first time cleared; all had set to work to scrub paint work and clean up ship. The dogs had made a rough looking mess of the deck; on account of the lumber, could not be cleaned up before.

It was pleasant all day, thermometer 34° above. We had lots of work in the engine department—eleven patches to go in the boiler, and four tubes to go in, and the whole department to clean up—the paint work in the engine-room was in a bad condition, the bilges to be cleaned up and lime to be put in them to keep off the horrid smell. Everyone at work. I had the day's duty; had fire on the donkey boiler.

Oct. 18th To-day commenced to send down light spars and rigging and stow them [away for the winter]. We had lots of work to do below. I bought some seal skins, well tanned for clothing, and a young deer skin for making liner for clothes. We ate pickled whale meat at dinner, and at supper tried the saurkraut. It may do for some, but I am not hungry enough yet to relish it, and hope I won't have to fall back on that kind of feed.

During the day, a party went off shooting. Mr. Stoney, Lane, Castillo and Morrison; they expected to remain away all night; some of the natives remained on board all night.

Oct. 19th The party remained off all night, so I took the day's duty in Morrison's stead. He don't often fail to be on hand when it is his duty, and I may want to be off some time. The party returned toward night and brought one duck. They had found a good harbor in a land locked bay, deep water and the place well supplied with seal. They reported that they had taken soundings, found six fathoms; no current. Plenty of ducks seen here. Captain Berry and Mr. Waring are to look at the place, and may decided to go there for winter quarters.

All day there were a lot of natives on board.

[*Oakland Tribune*] The Tchoutkichis lived in domed huts made of walrus skin.

The greatest chief in this part of the country visited us. We entertained him in our room; he was pleased with the pictures in "Frank Leslie's" Magazine, as a child would be. I gave him sugar and hard bread; he brought a lot of his chums with him to share his feast. We had singing and DeTracy played on the cornet.

A heavy fog came up at night, many of the natives stayed on board. Chief's name is OMLITHEOTH. [In subsequent entries, this chief's name is given as Omlithcot.]

Oct. 20th To-day heavy winds commence, and before night it was blowing quite hard, so we hurried up on the boiler; had to work late; got all the plates on, and grate bars in; the ship was crowded with natives, it was too rough for them to go on shore. Men, women, and children come here, day after day, and sit on the deck getting what they can to eat. We give them all we can, but there are so many of them, that some of them have to go hungry. Among the men some of them can speak English enough to be understood. Many of them have been on whale ships one or two seasons. They are very inquisitive, ask how many men, rifles, big guns; how much powder and lead we have; how much feed there is on board, and are entirely puzzled about this ship; it is not a whaler or a trade vessel—the only kinds of ships they have any idea of. It makes us feel a little squirmish to see such a lot of natives take note of everything so minutely. There are hundreds of them in the neighborhood, some desperate men; and at Pt. Barrow a lot of them made an attempt to take a whaler, but fell through on the job.

Oct. 21st Wind increasing; let go the right bower anchor and it kept us from drifting. We all worked late on the boiler, as it might soon be necessary, it the wind came up, to run the engine. It was found the soft coal was all used up, to run the engine. I am glad of it, and hope we will get no more of it. We had taken out the bad tubes, and I don't think we will have time to get them in. Hard work gives us a good appetite, but I wish the rush was over.

Oct. 22nd The wind increased, and orders to get boiler together and get up steam. We had to plug up the holes where the tubes had been removed. Everything finished, we ran the water into the boiler and got up steam. All night, with both anchors to hold, we steamed against the wind; the ship was not dragging the anchors, but for some reason it was thought best to run and trip them up occasionally. The sail and rigging that had been sent down was stowed in the coal

73

bunkers. Quite a lot of the ship's stores were removed amidship, to trim ship, as she was down by the head. The house built on the upper deck for reading room for the men, was now used for a workshop; the days are fast getting short; the sun sets AT 4 P.M. All night the gale continued. Natives went on the spit to-day in the canoes; turned the canoes over and slept under them.

Oct. 23rd Steamed all day against heavy gale. Some spars and sail were sent down from aloft. In the afternoon a hurricane; again all we could do to keep our anchorage. Quite a lot of trouble in our mess about the scarcity of food; no dinner to-day; that has often been the case lately. I don't care; two meals is all I have eaten a day since I came from Frisco. Men now expect as many meals as when they got up at 4 A.M. and turned in at 10 P.M. Ever since we started, this mess has had its regular daily growl, many time nearly coming to blows; of course, the other men is to blame, we all think. I wish I had gone along with the sailors when they asked me; I should have gotten along as well and had a better opinion of these companions.

Oct. 24th Wind went down some to-day. The natives on the beach kept looking to the ship; it was thought they wanted something to eat; they had been about sixty hours without any food. Some of the sailors put some meat and bread into a barrel, and lowered it overboard; the wind was blowing to the spit, and it soon reached the shore; it didn't take them long to knock the head of the barrel in, and find the provisions, which they quickly ate. It was then reported to the Captain, that the natives on the spit were hungry. He ordered some bread, meat, and molasses to be sent in to them. Three sailors volunteered to go in with the food in the dinghy, and food for the dogs. A long line was fastened to the boat and she went in shore, and landed provisions for the natives and dogs. The men got wet through launching the boat against the wind and spray. The natives were very thankful and were told that they were to get food until they could go to their village. Toward night the wind went down, and it began to snow; we stopped steamer and had a rest, and all night in. London sick.

Oct. 25th Wind came up again and had to run the engine. The natives came to the ship. I had cut a sealskin pants, and one of the women came in our mess and showed me how to sew the seams and gave me some deer skin thong thread. We fed the natives on board, and sent stuff to those on shore. The wind dies out at times, then we would stop steaming. It was cold, so steam was turned on the heaters; one of the native girls, about ten years old, scrubbed the floor and her face.

Oct. 26th Quite cold. Steam on heaters all day. Natives on board; I got the women to sew on pants and sea skin cap, lined with deerskin; they like to be down in the warm engine room. I wish the ice would form around, it seems as if we were not

74

to get frozen in this month. London sick.

Oct. 27ᵗʰ Steam on the heater, and the engine run. We stand our regular watch, night and day now, and will until the ice forms around, or we go into winter quarters. More stores were gotten up from below; it is a good thing for the crew when provisions are taken from the forehold and piled around the forecastle; lots of stores moved aft. The ship has been thoroughly cleaned. On deck, for a long time, the water closet, that never has been of much use, has been closed up; making it bad for the crew. Work on fur clothing as cold weather is here.

Oct. 28ᵗʰ The crew were all day trimming ship. One of the natives that we had with us has gotten back from his furlough; he was well pleased with the presents given him by the Captain, but wants six fathoms of calico. There is no end to the many wants of these people; if they see an old tin can or other useless article, to them it is of great use, and we all save such stuff for them.

Oct. 29ᵗʰ Quite pleasant to-day. Went in on the spit; had Mr. Lane's skates; DeTracey and I had a big time skating for the first time; the natives saw skating for the first time and tried to outrun us.

Oct. 29ᵗʰ The Captain and party went in shore to shoot a mess of ducks and returned with a few. The natives had a piece of black skin on board; it was smelling very old, but they ate it. It is pleasant weather to-day, but at this time of the year it is changeable and the wind comes suddenly. All spars and light sails are down below. I made a new baking pan, with cover, for beans.

Oct. 30ᵗʰ Banked fires, and have to steam as the wind increases. Captain Berry and party go on shore to-day; bring a big hogshead; it is to be set up in the marsh where the game is plenty, so a man can shoot them as they fly over.

All my fur clothes are done, so I put them on to try them; they smell like a fieldhand wedding; they are very warm and the wind does not go through them as it does through the best of our cloth.

Oct. 31ˢᵗ My day's duty—cleaning up Department as well as we can with steam on to-day. Each officer and all of the crew had buffalo mittens and cap served out to them to-day; they are well made and very warm. My week as caterer commences; I make it a rule to have plenty of baked beans and corn bread on hand, it is good food to fill up on, and stops the everlasting growling in our mess. The caterer has quite a lot of work to do making up biscuits and corn bread, soak and bake beans, set the table, wash up and put away dishes, keep the dish towels clean, draw all provisions, sweep up and, once a week, scrub paint work and floor. The caterer has to stand quite a lot of fault finding, and has one week in five to serve. (I wish it were a month.)

Nov. 1st Have winds again, so we have to steam. Nearly all day a man, in part European costume, seen on the beach; supposed to be the other native that has been off on a visit home. He continued to make signs to us, but it was too rough to lower a boat, so he returned in the direction of north. Head wind kept up all night.

Nov. 2nd Steamed all day; this wind may last weeks yet, but when it does stop, we are to up anchor and go nearer shore.

To-day I made bread pans for the sailors, and got some yeast bread. I have all the tinsmithing to do and kept busy most of the time. I am going to study arithmetic this winter, but if all hands find as many jobs for me as they have done lately, I will be just so much out.

This bread made forward is quite good, so we give the cook our flour.

Nov. 3rd Wind is dying out. Captain and Mr. Waring look at the harbor found by Mr. Stoney and Zane and decide not to go there. Fox traps are set on shore near a lot of fox holes. There are plenty of fox and rabbit in the country and natives catch a great many every season. They make shirts of rabbit skin and line clothes with fox skin; also make under shirts. The hunters did not catch any game.

Nov. 4th Messrs. Waring and Stoney went in shore early this morning to shoot ducks; they traveled as far as north head and back; got some ducks.

All hands called up to anchor, then we went in near the shore and anchored; it is a more sheltered place; at noon DeTracey, Gardner, Hodgson and I went in with the dinghy. We all wanted a run on the beach; there was quite a heavy wind at the time, and often quite a spray washed over us; finally we reached the shore; the boat was beached and anchored and Mr. DeTracey scored two nice ducks. Afterward we ran up the hill; here we came to the graves of white sailors, that had died at this bay. On the rough board sunk at each head was whittled their names; not date or mention of where they were from; they were whale men. Here, also, we found the wreck of the Whaler, "Cleone"; the vessel was full of oil; came in here during a storm, parted her anchors and was driven in shore and went to pieces. After going up the beach, we met Waring and Stoney returning; came back and pulled them out to the ship; didn't get much of a run on shore, after all my trouble, but was tired and slept well.

Nov. 5th Today the order was passed that the ship was to be put in order for winter quarters; the fire on the main boiler was hauled, and the fire started on the donkey boiler to heat ship. Bush was added to the list of firemen; we commenced to disconnect pipes in the engine room, put on blank flanges; scale and clean the main boiler, clean up the department generally. I was set at work on a new alcohol stove for sledge parties.

Nov. 6th To-day men worked on the tubes; I was on the job; it was thought best by the engineer to have everything in readiness, in case we had to run again on account of wind. The main steam pipe was taken down, new joints made, and it was replaced. Orders to remove the steam trap from the lower engine room to a place in the hold, where we filled the tanks. It required quite a lot of piping to make this change, and we have used up about all the spare pipe brought from Frisco. I get let in for all piping jobs, and with that kind of work, tin repairing, stove work, and odd jobs for the officers and men, about all my time is used up. The furnaces and boiler are to be painted, the boiler room white-washed, upper engine room scrubbed and painted and lime sprinkled in the bilge. It will take weeks to do this, as we have had no good opportunity before this, to clean up. The whole place is very dirty; we work from 8:30 A.M. until 5 P.M.; one hour at noon for dinner and smoking.

Nov. 7th Heavy wind to-day. A party was sent in shore to feed the dogs on the spit; had a time landing, the surf coming in heavy on the beach. When we came to launch the boat found great trouble; the men got wet; Burch and London had their fingers frozen. One of the natives came to the beach, where the boat had been driven after leaving the spit. London's feet were wet and fast freezing—Sam, as the native is called, took off his dry stockings and gave them to London to save his feet, and suffered the cold rather than see this man lose the use of his feet. The men had their mittens and boots wet, their coats all stiff—no fur clothing has been distributed; the rats are fast destroying it. Many of the men, when they are ordered into the boat, are not sufficiently clothed and must suffer. The boat was left on the beach, and men went into the dinghy afterward; boat towed to ship in bad condition.

Nov. 8th DeTracey and Quirk are working on a sled; it is a fine piece of work. To-day I put up the piping to steam box to bend the runners and seat.

Nov. 9th Quite cold to-day—work going on in the engineer's department and on the sled. Fixed valve in the forecastle; worked on a tin-box for Mr. Stoney and on an alcohol stove designed by Captain Berry. DeTracey repaired Hunt's shoes.

Nov. 10th To-day the preparations were commenced for to send a party to communicate with Mr. Putnam at Cape Sergkaman [a distance of about thirty miles overland]—Mr. Hunt with Schuman and London are to go with the sled and nine dogs. Morgan and Bruch are making a tent; Quirk is making tent poles; they expect to camp out, and are to take twelve days' provisions with them. Captain Berry and Mr. Waring ordered the boat to go duck hunting—they came all dressed up warm in furs and remarked to the men in the boat dressed in navy clothes, that they were not dressed warm enough. The men would willingly have taken a suit of government clothes made of furs, if they were issued, but they did not like to be asking for them; certainly it was very cold in an open boat, and the wind up here, at this time of year, goes through a navy coat to the body in a short time; and once cold it takes a good fire to thoroughly warm a man up again. No ducks shot to-day—boat hauled up—men turned in.

Nov. 11th Work going on in the engineer's department, and on tent. The new sled is nearly done—quite cold to-day.

Nov. 13th [There is no Nov. 12th in Cahill's typed manuscript] Work going on in all departments to help fix things up for winter. I put steam pipe to the bath tub; the men are to wash clothes here in cold weather—and clothes lines are put up to dry wet and damp clothes. The room is kept warm all the time, as steam is now kept up night and day on the donkey boiler.

Nov. 14th I am kept busy at work on alcohol stoves of the Captain's design—they are to be used by parties that go on short journeys, to melt snow for drinking and cooking purposes; as yet the right thing has not been found. Morrison has to see to the cleaning of the department; Gardner and I, when our day's duty comes, look out for repairs and donkey boiler. DeTracey's work, to run the mess; and he makes the worst sort of a caterer, and I am glad when he gets through; I depend upon the pantry when he swings a big hammer, yet he thinks he does it first-class.

Nov. 15th Captain and party go to the spit to hunt ducks and plover, and the men to feed the dogs. One of the dogs has been killed and eaten, and another killed and is partly eaten up. These dogs get fits and act as if they were dizzy, running around in a circle; the other dogs then pile onto them and kill them and afterwards eat them. The dogs are not properly taken care of—for several days men cannot get to the spit to feed them; so they kill one another—they ate a young dog we got at St. Michaels, named Bootleg, as fine a fellow as any of them.

The Captain's party did get a few ducks this time; men get back to the ship cold and hungry.

Nov. 16th The party that are sent to Mr. Putnam are now ready, weather permitting, to go to the Cape. On shore the snow is soft. Mr. Hunt has never done any sled work, and although he may make a good hand at it—it is the opinion,

78

among the natives and the men who have talked with them, that the snow is not hard enough for traveling, and that they will never reach Cape Sergkaman—but he has to start tomorrow—the load is put on the sled, and with the sled weighs 450 lbs.—nine dogs are to haul the load. None of the men ever drove dogs before, the men going are weighed to see if they lose much by traveling—pemmican for men and dogs is the principal food; they are take a direct course by compass to the Cape.

At night the men in the forecastle have one of their jubilee concerts—harmonicas, bones and singing; they have quite a good time forward, and make the time fly along. The firemen work the most hours at present, until the cleaning is done in the Engine Department.

Nov. 17th Quite stormy to-day, yet Mr. Hunt and men are to make a start for Cape Sergkaman; the sled and dogs are put into the whale boat; the Captain goes in to see him start the dinghy, and brings some of the stuff on shore. Both boats find trouble in landing; finally all get safely on shore. The Captain's boat returns to the ship, leaving Mr. Hunt to start; it is found after a few hours that the dogs and men cannot bring so heavy a load, and Mr. Hunt thinks if he can get more men, he will be alright. He decides to return in the dinghy to the ship, and have another talk and sleep—now to reach the ship with the dinghy; the wind was ahead; two men only left to bring her off—Bruch and Johansen. They had to haul her along the beach until they got about a mile up, so that they could run down on the ship, which they have done.

Mr. Hunt talked with the Captain and instead of getting more men, it was thought best to reduce the size and weight of the load. Schuman and London on shore put up the tent, cooked some coffee, turned in; the snow falling and in no way fit to start on a sled journey. Quite a lot of trouble now ahead, giving out the lime juice; we don't get it at any regular time of day—when they think it will give the most trouble; some men take it, others don't. It is time something was done about fixing a water closet; the men have no convenience either sick or well, and though all complain, yet nothing is yet thought of being done. This putting off everything until we get frozen in is a bad thing for us; we may not freeze in this winter. Several times the ice has come and gone.

Nov. 18th Mr. Hunt made another start to-day; the load reduced to 315 lbs., the tent and stuff put on to the sled; the snow soft and it was quite late when the party got off, about 10:30 A.M—we watched them from the ship until they were out of sight. I think it would be better, if they took natives to guide and help them —the men had on show shoes. Schuman and London had sealskin pants that they had traded for; Mr. Hunt's suit was mostly government furs. It was not very cold; we worked on stoves and cleaning up; department men are kept busy; as yet, no move has been made to open the reading room; there is reading matter enough on board. We send from our mess all books we read, up forward, and they seldom come back—I have read quite a lot of Swedenborg's, and like his arguments; read Lakeside novels, and several of Marryatt's works—think they are far behind the wants of to-day.

Nov. 19th Very little going on to-day. Too cold to do much around deck; men are gathering snow; we run short of water, and the changes are we will have to fire up the main boiler to condense water and fill the tanks; it is hardly possible to keep up the supply of water now required, with the fixings we have for melting snow. The cooks have been notified to use the water very sparingly—it comes hard on many not yet used to it and living on a small lot of water. But before winter we may get used to this thing; very little washing is done now, and the chances are there will be less.

Nov. 20th Men sent on shore to feed dogs; lots of heavy ice drifting, and it freezes in the mush ice; while they were on shore, after feeding the dogs, there was lots of trouble getting the boat to a place where it could be floated off—the men had to drag it a long way up the beach, and when they at last found a place to get through the ice, it was found necessary to cut the way and work very carefully, as young ice cuts as a knife—it took them a long time to reach the ship.

Nov. 21st Captain and party go on shore again to shoot ducks; the ice has moved away again. After they had gone, two seals were seen on the ice—Morrison and Hodgson went off in the canoe, with rifles and spear to catch one of the seals; they got quite close to him, and fired at him several times; the seal looked up at him, from his peaceful sleep, to see if he was the one they were firing at, but when he saw Hodgson, he knew he could take another sleep, as he never accomplished what he started for; then they paddled up till quite near, and the seal went off into the water. The other seal had drifted within shot, and DeTracey fired and hit him. A boat was lowered and it was taken on board; it was not a large one; it was breathing hard, and Mr. Zane fired into it a shot from his revolver Huebner and Hodgson skinned it. As usual, something must happen; Hodgson went to was a big part of the seal overboard and, not securing it right, it went over board and sank. The stomach of the seal was full of tape worms. We ate seal meat cooked—I like it. Some was kept for Thanksgiving. Captain's party shot quite a lot of ducks.

Nov. 22nd Had heavy snow last night, and early this morning, men commenced to gather it to melt it for washing and to supply the donkey boiler; it is shoveled into boxes and carried to the donkey boiler room. There must be some arrangement made soon for melting show, or we will have to start up the main boiler. The work on it is all done: it has been cleaned inside and cleaned and painted on the outside and in the connections and furnaces; all the hand and manhole plates are off; so is the feed pipe from the Kingston; all the main steam pipe has been taken down, new joints made and the pipe put up again; pipes from the injection and outboard delivery valves are removed and put away; blank flanges have been put on. The engine room is now scrubbed, the lower engine room painted and whitewashed; the bilges have been cleaned and lime sprinkled in them. Very little work now remains to be done in the department. Pumps have been overhauled, new packing put in, and joints made.

To-day warning one of the firemen; got a lecture from the Chief for being saucy; the blacksmith was sent to the mast and also straightened out. The crew have long been doing just about as they please. An order was passed not to burn candles or open lights after 8 P.M., which the men don't like. [Acting Boatswain] Morgan seems to have very little control of the men. He is a good sailor, but can neither read nor write, and has had trouble ever since we left Frisco. Cold to-day; no one leaves the ship.

Nov. 23rd Ice broke away again, and men go in with the officers to shoot a mess of ducks for the great Thanksgiving we expect; some ducks that have been killed are being saved. None of our mess have been out to shoot lately; we have been kept busy; DeTracey, our Nimrod, is building a sled; Morrison looks after cleaning up in the department; Gardner thinks it is too cold; I am kept busy on the new stoves, and Hodgson is having his week to run the mess. This is the first time since we have been out that he has done it to satisfy the mess, but I must say we get two quite good meals every day now. I intend to ask Mr. Waring for some ducks, if any are caught. We had quite a talk in the mess, and all hands have to help fix up a Thanksgiving feed. Joe is and Englishman and, as yet, don't know how to enjoy life, unless there is liquor to brighten up his ideas. We have had quite a time listening to his many adventures; he has been up her in every whaler that ever left San Francisco, and steered "Thil Orme" two seasons; that is glory enough to retire on, but we found him in Frisco, after all the whalers had gone North; our poet has rubbed him up with his bold actions; and still we hear of whales. The party on shore got lots of ducks; I got three big ones for our mess. Ice forming again around the ship, and quite cold.

Nov. 24th I have the day's duty; have to make a new lot of bread pans, and I have made a new, covered bean pan for our mess, giving our old one to the Captain's steward. We have saved up part of our rations, and, if eating will make a Thanksgiving, we certainly have enough for one day. Gardner, DeTracey and I pick the ducks, Joe cleans them and prepares them, also mixes the stuffing; it just takes a lot of hungry men to mix up a feed. I mad a lot of corn bread and we eat the biggest part of it before supper; we have a good supply of coffee and tea; always rather short of flour; there is lots of cheese rotting among the stores, but, as yet, none has been issued, except to the officers. Men are let off from work quite early to-day, and no work on board to-morrow. Card playing and reading take up the evening. We have a new table in our mess; it is quite a nuisance—it squeaks if one leans on it and don't fill the want. Our room is twelve feet long, eight feet deep, seven feet high; five men sleep here at times; some think too little air, some too much; some want steam on, others don't; DeTracey gets sick if the window is open—Hodgson can't sleep if it is shut; so we have lots of fun. I go to bed early about 7 P.M., get up at 6 A.M.—the rest want to lie in till daylight; I go out and get my coffee and hard tack, when I can; then light up lamp and read till breakfast time. We work from daylight till 5 P.M., breakfast at 8:30, supper at 5:15 P.M.

Nov. 25th Thanksgiving. Up early this morning and at work on the day's cooking; I made biscuits for breakfast—came out good; soon all the baking powder will be used up—then we will have a time. We have had a few messes of bread made with saleratus—it is only a waste of flour. Had quite a good feed at breakfast; no work to-day; men are taking it easy—it is not often they get a holiday, not even a Sunday. Gardner thinks if he were home he would be in for a dance to-night, and the rest of the men think of turkey. The ducks were passed to the cook early, and, with fruit and a cake, that I got from the pantry, some canned oysters, raisins, seal meat, soup, and a few other things we are to have a big blow out. Supper comes on early, no hurry, and a good feed; everyone is satisfied for once. In the evening we have some music—DeTracey works the cornet, and we have a good accordion. I turn in early; DeTracey and Morrison sit up and argue on religion, morals, and a few other subjects, till the light burns out. They have quite a good time in the forecastle; the men take the evening for a concert and keep it up quite late. To-night in the cabin, the officers have a big supper, and sit up late, telling of how they have spent the day in other places. It has been very cold all day; ice is around, and it was lucky for us that we got our ducks so early, as none are seen when the Bay is frozen over.

Nov. 26th To-day the ice moved off and left quite a clear space. Captain Berry thought best, as the dogs were fast destroying each other, to have them taken on board. The boat is sent into the spit and the men make a landing; with food they entice the hungry dogs, and succeed in catching nearly all of them. One takes to the water, and the men follow him up and finally catch him; most of them are as wild as a pack of wolves. We are sorry to have the dogs on board—they are a great nuisance; the boat reaches the ship all right; the dogs that are not caught are left some food.

Nov. 27th Boat again sent out to-day; quite cold and stiff breeze; men take the shot guns and get a few ducks. When returning, the wind was blowing quite hard, and the boat's mast was carried away; there were lively times fixing up and pulling to the ship; all got on board in safety. Lately when boats are lowered, it is found very difficult to work the center board, as it freezes in the box.

Nov. 28th Open water and mush ice—some snow; it was cold last night and all to-day. A big hogshead has been fitted up on the fore passage to melt the ice and snow; I run the steam pipe into it, connecting with the main from the donkey boiler; it is filled with snow to try it, and we find it better to let the steam strike the snow from the top; it melts it quicker. All the clean snow collected is melted and run down into the tanks. It takes a big lot of snow to make a few gallons of water; but snow is falling very often now, and we expect to get enough without going on shore for it. About dark, the quarter-master on watch saw a light on shore, signaling to the ship. A boat was lowered at once and sent in. It was found to be Mr. Hunt and the men who started for Cape Sergkaman; they were badly used up with useless traveling, and reported having had a tough time of it.

Mr. Hunt's excursion between St. Lawrence Bay and East Cape; leaving the place where Schuman and London had camped all night, with the load on sled reduced from four hundred fifty to three hundred fifteen pounds, the men started, and for three days followed a course north and west; then came a lot of mountains, too high to be gotten over with the heavy load. At night they camped and, after meeting the mountain range, followed it along till they came out at East Cape, instead of Kalucien Bay, where they expected to be. The bad sledging and weather kept them dragging around until the ninth day; then they had used up most of the provisions, and killed a dog, "Baby", one of the youngest we got at Petropaulovski; this was eaten, and part given to the dogs.

Finally they reached North Head; then they did what they should have done at the start, that is, to have taken the advice and guidance of the natives, who certainly know how to get along in their own country. The men rested one night and, in the morning, started for the ship. Three natives, Sam, Shoofly and Setzmar, came out to the ship with them; having helped the men to the vessel, the natives came on board, where they were fed; they stayed on board all night—they came to our quarters and ate some hard tack and molasses. I bought some sealskin boots from Setzmar for one plug of tobacco, and got a nice pair of fancy worked women's boots, that I am to take home—they are a fine specimen of work, considering what these people have to work with.

Hunt's party found a dead "Masinka Man" in the snow.

Nov. 29th Had day's duty to-day, and worked on the alco-stove; the cleaning up is now nearly finished—then we expect to get a rest for a few weeks; the work on the ship has kept us busy in our department. DeTracey and Quirk have finished the sled and the natives that came to the ship with Mr. Hunt are tying it with deer thongs, the best fastenings—lots of trouble finding a knot that holds. Quite cold to-day; no snow; ice gone away again from the ship.

8. Fire!

Nov. 30th Early this morning, the fireman relieving at 8 A.M. noticed smell of smoke in the donkey boiler room, and it was noticed about 8 A.M. in the forecastle; inquiries were made, and search was begun for its cause; at 8:45 A.M. smoke came up the pipe from the chain locker, and Morgan went aft and reported the ship on fire in the forehold. Immediately all hands were called to save ship; the fire pumps had been disconnected to keep them from freezing, and the carpenter and others at once went to work on them to connect them; hot water was let down to get them to suck.

At the time steam was on the donkey boiler to heat ship, and here was connected with Sewall pump; very soon a good stream was thrown into the forehold, where, at this time, the smoke was fast rushing. Morgan had a line attached to him, and he went down and guided the hose till driven up by the smoke. Although relieved by Bruch and others, the smoke had so increased that the fireman was driven from the boiler room and steam at once began to go down.

It was very necessary to keep up steam, so Captain Berry ordered the carpenter to cut a hole in the deck, over the donkey boiler, then Morrison, McCarthy and I took turns in being lowered down through this hole in the deck, with wood to feed the boiler fire. Finally the water in the tank that supplies the boiler was used up, and it also got so smokey in the boiler room that no one could venture into it.

I made a proposal to get up steam in the main boiler, as we could do it in a few hours, and if we kept the fire in check that time with the fire pump, it was expected to put it out with two streams from the Sewall pump. Mr. Zane, with the three machinists and our fireman, went to the fire room, and at once commenced to get the boiler closed up. We had been cleaning, scaling and painting it. Besides there were several new tubes put in and some new patches just put on, the man and hand hole plates were off, the pipe connecting the boiler and Kingston valve was removed, grate bars cut. The boiler, with all these disadvantages, was closed up, water run in and a head of steam to run the Sewall pump with two good streams—in less than two and a half hours from the time we started on it.

While this work was going on in our department, Captain Berry ordered the anchors to be slipped and buoyed; this was done.

For a time it seemed as if we were gaining on the fire, but it finally drove the men from between decks; then the hatchways were battened down and sail made to run the ship into shallow water to scuttle her. I was ordered to break a joint in the main steam pipe, that led to the hoisting engine in the forecastle; after considerable trouble, I broke a joint in the pipe through the hole cut out in the deck over the donkey boiler; three lengths of suction hose were connected and fastened; one end was securely fastened to the opening in the pipe, bound with canvas; the other end led to the forehold. The proposition to use steam was from me, and I told Captain Berry that I had seen it used in a cotton factory, with the best results; then steam was turned on from the main boiler to this hose, and a hose was led to the forecastle with streams of water; and a stream kept up from the Sewall pump led to the forehold.

Morgan worked so hard that he gave out and was carried aft for treatment. Grace, also, stayed guiding the hose between decks till too much smoke he swallowed laid him out. McCarthy had a sore throat form smoke; he was the last man to give up firing the donkey boiler. Bruch, McShane, Berk and Lloyd worked hard all the time we were able to fight the fire. When I was breaking the joint in the steam pipe, I had not the strength to start the union, and asked Captain Berry for a man to help me; Mr. Stoney volunteered his assistance.

I was, at the time, part way reaching down to the pipe, through the hole cut in the deck; the pipe wrench in my hand—Mr. Stoney stumbled and fell on me, and, to save myself, I braced back against the deck; my back was hurt; Mr. Stoney was called away, and Bruch came and helped me till the hose was connected. I went aft to see Doctor Castillo—found him in his bunk; I told him of my hurt; he could do nothing—advised me to take a little fresh air or go off and let him rest.

Nearly all the men had sore throats from smoke. The pump on deck was manned early in the day, and kept up a stream till near night when the men, having eaten no food since breakfast, were too tired to move; they were ordered for other work. Coffee was issued to all hands about 11 A.M. The three natives on board, that came out with Mr. Hunt, worked at the pumps and wherever they were asked, from beginning of the fire till we were ordered to abandon ship. They were promised calico, tobacco and many things they ought to get.

The day was very cold and ice had formed around the ship; and it was very slow she moved through it, to the shallow water near the mainland; but, finally, she grounded in about three fathoms of water. The chief engineer and Morrison fastened the outboard delivery valve open by means of a line that led to the poop deck through the ash shoot. This let in a stream of six inches in diameter, and with the water that had been pumped I since morning, it was soon to the grate bars and put out the fire in the main boiler.

During a short interval of rest the men had about this time, we got together a few clothes; no fur clothing, except caps and mittens, had been issued to the men—the officers had fur clothing.

We were then ordered to launch the boats, and every man that was able to do anything took hold; all the boats were gotten over, and the officers and men got the few clothes they had saved into their boats. There was some pemican, flour, beans, sugar, and coffee, enough for fifteen days' rations, saved and got into the boats; no one was detailed to save provisions during the early part of the day —there was open water, and a few boatloads might have been landed; one can of hard tack was got into the boat; we also saved nine rifles, four shotguns, cartridges, powder, a box of trade stuff, canvas, bale of blankets, bale of drawers, and bale of stockings.

Morrison and Gardner each saved their Winchester rifles, with reloading apparatus, and about five hundred shells and three hundred extra bullets. Mr. DeTracey lost a Winchester rifle and double-barreled shotgun, half a box of tobacco, some matches and all the money in the safe; no medicine saved—no fire near dispensary.

After the ship had grounded and was scuttled, an anchor was got over to hold her; Bruch, Lloyd, Quirk and I got it over the bow—a bale of flannel was also saved.

The mush ice had formed around the ship; it was very deep but not solid enough to stand on yet—too stiff to run a boat through. Mr. Waring sent Morrison, Berk and Smith on shore with the skin canoe; they had to take boards to stand on and lift the canoe over the ice, then get into the canoe, and move the boards to the front, and so on. They carried with them an axe and small line. Finally they reached the shore, and a heavy line was made fast to their small line and hauled in shore, then made fast to a very secure rock.

The idea of going over the mush ice this way was Berk's. The boats were got in line, ready to go on shore; Mr. Stoney's boat took the lead, Mr. Zane in the dinghy next, Mr. Waring next, then Captain Berry's boat, and the last boat in charge of Mr. Hunt—I was in that boat. At 11:40 P.M. Captain Berry ordered all the officers and men to their boats—while we were in the Arctic, the men had been told which was their boat and place, in case we had to abandon ship. The powder and coal oil were on deck, and two men from Mr. Hunt's boat were ordered on board again by Mr. Hunt; Lloyd and Johansen went up and throw over powder, oil, and some fireworks; O'Leary and I pulled into our boat four of the fifty-pound boxes of powder and quite a lot of coal oil. The fire kept increasing and it looked risky to be on the ship.

[*Oakland Tribune*] Captain Berry ordered all hands ashore, but one of the men wanted to remain on board the *Rodgers* to recover what clothing he could for use in the long winter that they must now all spend on shore. The captain in a rage shouted, "The first man who dares disobey my commands will be shot down!" Seaman Lloyd obeyed.

Captain Berry ordered the men to get into the boats; Johansen got in—Lloyd was still hunting up stuff, though ordered to the boat; Captain Berry told Mr. Hunt to knock him overboard, but Lloyd got into the boat; the Mr. Hunt came down, the last man to leave the "Rodgers."

Dec. 1st The boats were pulling in by the line, not making much headway; the ice was fast getting hard—some of the men got out and tried to stand on it, but had to get into the boats again; the three natives got out with paddles and, on their hands and knees, went in till near the beach where the ice got soft; they were picked up by the boat and skin canoe, that came out again. At last Mr. Stoney's boat reached the shore, making and opening through the ice and leaving it easier for the other boats to follow.

At about half past one, the fire broke through on the starboard bow. It was betting very warm in our boat; we had, as yet, made so very little headway; Captain Berry ordered us to get into the boat ahead of us, his boat, and make our boat fast to the long line. Lloyd misunderstood the order, as Mr. Hunt gave it; the line was fastened on board the ship, and to fasten our boat to it, without cutting it adrift from the ship, meant to leave our clothes in the boat and abandon her.

The men in our boat had gone down in the forecastle, at the time of the fire, and, at the risk of their lives had got out their bags; so Lloyd was for saving the boat and its contents, and told Mr. Hunt it was easy to order to leave the boat as he (Mr. Hunt) had all his clothes and stuff in the boat that went ahead. Lloyd went back, after fastening the boat's painter to the line, and cut the line on the other side of the fastening, leaving it free to hail in the boat if we reached the shore; it took time to do this, and Lloyd argued the point with Mr. Hunt. Captain Berry told Lloyd he would shoot him, and asked Mr. Hunt to knock Lloyd in the head. We were then ordered to get forward into Mr. Waring's boat, fastening the second last boat, also, to the line. Captain Berry dropped out of his pocket into the mush ice, a box containing two valuable rings—this happened while he was speaking to Lloyd.

After getting into the forward boats, as there were more of us to pull, we made much better headway, and the boats reached the shore then we hauled the two remaining boats in by the line. Then all the boats were discharged, hauled upon the beach and the beds and clothing got into them. All the boats in shore and hauled up at half past two.

[*Oakland Tribune*] In all, nine rifles, four shotguns, some bales of trade stuff, some canvas, blankets, drawers and stockings had been saved. Cahill, exhausted from the fight against the fire, threw himself face-down on the beach, heedless of the cold and wind.

The fire had been increasing all the time and now the whole ship was in a blaze. Some dogs, that had been taken on board a few days before, were seen running about the deck, and they finally jumped on the ice. The men made up beds and, after the hard day's work and having had very little to eat, most of them turned in.

It was a grand sight, one long to be remembered by us who witnessed it, to see the burning vessel; thousands of cartridges were stored in the hold, and, as the fire reached them, they were exploded. Steam was not blowing off from the main and donkey boilers, the fire room and decks being in a blaze; the fire was running up the rigging; masts, yards and sail were in a blaze; the reports when oil, alcohol, or powder was exploded, and sheets of flame sweeping the entire length of the ship—all helped to make a grand picture. Captain Berry and a few of the men stay awake all night to watch the fire. About 3:30 the line on the anchor over the bow parted, and the ship commenced to drift as she lightened up. The wind was increasing and, as the ship floated from the shallow water, she moved off toward South Head.

The men lay in the boats; it was very cold; many had to get up and walk to keep the blood in circulation. At 6 A.M. we began to turn out and light fires on the beach; then pemican was opened and distributed; I got a can of Boston baked beans and a can of bartlett pears. Both were frozen stiff. Gardner looked the most forlorn that I could see; I called him and we went away from the crowd and ate the canned stuff, cutting it up with our sheath-knives. After daylight we melted snow and got some coffee; about noon I found a walrus buried on the beach, and cut off enough raw meat for my dinner; others soon found that raw walrus could be eaten, now that we had no other food.

During the morning, the ship drifted off toward South Head; about noon, two whale boats and the dinghy were launched, with all their load, and an attempt was made to reach North Head; but the ice again formed fast, and Mr. Waring decided to return. This time we landed farther down on the beach; the boat were unloaded and hauled up, far in on the beach, then turned over, and all the stuff stowed away. Afterwards all the bedding was brought under the boats and spread out; after eating some pemican, coffee was give out—then we turned in; there were thirty of us in this small space, and by keeping our clothes on and lying close together, we kept quite warm. During the night it snowed.

We had saved about twelve days' provisions altogether. After landing the boats, we tried to get two dogs on shore; they saw us on shore and started up the beach, but the soft ice let them into the water, and they returned to the heavy ice near the ship. The last we saw of them, at night, they were still near the burning ship.

Dec. 2ⁿᵈ Up early this morning and, from the remarks of the officers and men, the prospects for the remainder of our stay in this country are not very cheering. Of late the natives had been so often to the ship, just to beg and loaf around, that they had worn out their welcome, and, in many cases, we had, at night, to send them on shore; they could, in a short time, eat up our four years' ration, if they got it. Now the tables were turned, and it remained to be seen what these Indian natives would do with us, and how they would treat us; they were many, we were very few, and had to depend altogether on their hospitality.

Before sunrise, the natives from the village of North head came with dog sleds, and Captain Berry, Mr. Waring and others had a talk with them. Many of them have been on whalers, and can talk some English. The three natives that had been on board the ship, during the fire, lived at North Head—they had returned to help us. Without any promise of payment at the time, the men told us they would take us to their huts, and as long as they had any walrus or seal meat, we should be fed—and have shelter from the dreadful weather. The offer was gladly accepted by Captain Berry—he told them that a relief ship would come to St. Lawrence Bay and bring them powder, knives, tin kettles, calico, beads, food, and such things as they need.

[*Oakland Tribune*] It was clear that these savage people possessed some of the noblest traits. The hunters were stalwart and brave, venturing out over the ice in all weathers to bring home food for the village. Many of them bore the marks of their efforts—the stubs of fingers lost to the cold, the scars and stumps of limbs sacrificed in mortal combat with the polar bear. Despite their desperation to provide enough for themselves to eat, the Tchoutchis were very generous toward the shipwrecked sailors with their limited supplies of food. Once when one of the shipwrecked sailors was in danger of losing a foot to frostbite, an Eskimo took the foot onto his own breast and warmed it back to life.

At once we commenced to break camp, and as the men felt better, one of them played "Home Sweet Home" on the accordion; we ate pemican and had some coffee; then the bedding and clothes were loaded on the dog sleds, and the men started for North Head. It was about six miles away from where we were, on the beach. The snow was not hard enough on the crust to sustain the weight of a man at all time; it made traveling extra hard. I had been transferred to the chief engineer's boat. As each boat's crew had one sled to carry their bedding and clothes, we were expected to help the dogs pull the load. Mr. Hunt and four men were left to take charge of the boats and provisions. Before leaving, the other two whale boats were hauled far inland and all their cargo taken in and put in them, to be taken at some future time.

Our sled was last to get away, and after we started, Morgan came and told Captain Berry he was not able to walk; Captain told him to get on the sled; we had only a few dogs and some one had to go on ahead, to lead them.

Our party—Captain Berry, Chief Engineer Zane, Dr. Castillo, Morgan, Hodgson, McShane, Smith, myself, and two natives—after proceeding about a mile, saw that, with Morgan on the sled, we were too heavily loaded; my bag and bed and one other bag were thrown off, into the snow. I told the native Ranaow that, if he would carry my blankets, he could keep my bed quilt; it was calico, and he wanted it. He took them on his back, and we made another start—but had to rest often. The snow in many places was more than two feet deep, and it soon tired us wading through it, dragging the sled. Sometimes the crust of snow would hold us up; Captain Berry was heavier than the rest of us, and would sink through the crust when we could walk on it.

Mr. Zane was soon played out; Dr. Castillo gave out before we were half way—he did not pull on the sled, as Captain Berry and the rest of us did. After half the journey, I began to get used up and got cramps in my legs—my back hurt me where Mr. Stoney fell on me, during the fire; nearly every one hundred yards, Captain Berry, Mr. Zane, Dr. Castillo, and I would throw ourselves down on the snow, alongside the sled, and rest a few minutes. Often, lying on our backs, heedless of how we exposed ourselves to cold—long before we reached the village, Captain Berry, Mr. Zane, Dr. Castillo, and I gave up the idea of ever being able to reach it without help.

Night was fast coming on, and it began to snow and blow. It was bad enough when we could see ahead of us, now it did look kind of useless to try to get on any further. Dr. Castillo had, for some time, been riding on the sled, on top of Morgan and the load. I had cramps so bad that I could walk no further; Captain Berry saw that I was used up; he came back for me and ordered the sled to wait. Dr. Castillo had to walk awhile; I got on and rode for half a mile, then tried walking again and let Captain Berry take my place on the sled—I think he was the worst used up man of the party. Then Mr. Zane and I tramped on slowly together; the natives cheered us up, telling us not to lay down, or else we would sleep and die. Only a little way on was the village, but we lay down, and if the place was in sight, we had not strength or wish to move any further just then. The captain again stopped the sled, and we had come to a down hill place—Mr. Zane and I sat on top of poor Morgan and got another lift. Then the natives lost the road—the wind driving the snow in our faces, we could not even see the track of the sleds that had gone ahead. If we had dogs belonging to the village, they would easily find the road, but our sled had the ship's dogs, and the road was new to them.

Then it was decided we could not go on, but stay out in the storm till help came back for us, from those that had gone on ahead. Mr. Zane asked me if I expected this kind of a trip when I shipped; he didn't, and had all the Arctic he wanted in his—so did I just then, as we sat there in the snow storm. We heard a dog bark on our left and cried out to direct the attention of the party to us; the sled with six dogs came, and it was one of the natives, that had carried one party in, and returned to help us. We were quite a way from the track, and he took Captain Berry on his sled, and the Captain promised to send us help as soon as he reached the village. But just as the sled was to start, Dr. Castillo got on and left us; we followed the track till the snow covered it up; we had to go very slowly, then got lost again. The native, Sam, was sick—too much smoke at the fire was the cause; he said he would go on and come with help. We followed, pulling the sled, and when we could, Mr. Zane and I took turns in getting on for a spell. About this time Dominick Booker came to us; he had been left by his party, and was wandering about in the snow. He was very fortunate to meet us, as we were the last party to get in—if he had not met with us, his chances for a night in the storm were good.

Again we braced up, and the native with us said, "Now only a little way"—perhaps he thought a mile was a little way; but we will remember that little way a long time. We came to a steep bank, and the village was just upon the hill opposite; the dogs were taken from the sled; Morgan had to get off—I helped him down the hill. Mr. Zane, Hodgson, McShane came down with the sled—such a rush as they made—and the whole load upset at the foot of the hill—some cuss words. I went on with Morgan, and after a little walk, not knowing how near we were to the hut, he asked me to help him back to where the sled was; I did so and Ranaow, the native, after helping to load the sled, took me up with him to the village. It was dark and snowing at the time; the sled followed, and the men put up at the same house with the Captain, till better provided for.

[*Oakland Tribune*] Now that the ship was gone, it would become necessary to quarter the men with the natives, a few in each of the small villages of the Masinkas. These were themselves accustomed to subsistence living through the winter, and their meager resources would have to be carefully managed to support the added population of thirty-three shipwrecked sailors and their Russian dog-driver. "We'll have to wait here until the whaling vessels come in the Spring," said Zane.

I went to Ranaow's hut; the snow was brushed off my clothes. I had worn a pair of rubber boots and pants—they got too heavy for me in the end and helped to use me up. My boots and pants I took off in the outer part of the hut; then I followed the native, crawling under the deerskin curtain to the only room the hut contained. All the inmates, three women, two men and four children were naked. It was very warm in this place, and the smell was sickening.

[*Oakland Tribune*] The two women and three children of Ranaow's extended family inside the yoronger insisted on closely examining Cahill and the entire kit he brought in with him. The two women he found to be "fat and ugly" but the third, perhaps fourteen years of age an as yet unadorned by the paint marks on her lips and cheeks that would indicate she was a wife. Weary from his efforts to survive the burning of the ship, he threw himself onto a pile of skins and fell asleep. Now he fell victim to the lice that were to bedevil the rest of his life ashore among the native people of Siberia. He tried anointing his skin with kerosene salvaged from the ship, but it only seemed to whet the appetite of the noxious pests, in time to become the bane of his life with the native people.

Nothing in his former life had prepared Patrick Cahill for the experience of coming in contact with the native Chook-Chis in their own simple homes. He first entered the "yarat" or outer hut, where the dogs lived. When he crawled under his host Ranaow's tent-flap and encountered nine naked adults and children. Their bodies and the flame of a blubber lamp rendered the close confines of the yoronger too warm for anyone but an American to consider wearing clothing. In time he came to learn that the natives considered that wearing clothing indoors rendered those same skin coverings unusable outside in the cold weather, from the accumulated moisture from sweat. Cahill was too weary to be embarrassed, but was sickened by the intolerable stench of these unwashed people.

I was told to remove my clothes and did so; then the cramps returned to my legs—I hadn't the strength to rub them, but the woman was told what the matter was, and at once rubbed my legs until I felt better. I put on my drawers, and then being very hungry, ate some walrus blubber and roots that tasted like potatoes. McCarty was in this hut; he had a very sore throat and could hardly whisper—he could not eat.

I lay down on some deerskin but could not sleep. Soon Hodgson came in and commenced to act like a ten-year-old. The people had a big tub without cover, and all in the hut used it all night for a water-closet, which made it very disagreeable; the room was ninety-five or one hundred degrees all night—size, twelve long, seven deep, and four and one-half high; one might sit up in it, but could not stand. I had not lain down a great while before I felt something crawling on my arm. I looked, and it was a big louse; before morning I had killed a great many of them.

Dec. 3rd We were all up early this morning; all night I had not slept; at four A.M. the first lot of frozen walrus and frozen weeds, like grass, were brought in, and I ate some. By promises I induced the native to go and bring in my bag, that had been thrown off the day before; I promised him tobacco, thread and a comfort. He started; it was quite stormy at the time. I was glad when he went out, as it let fresh air come into the room. About 9 A.M. I got on some clothes and went out to see how the other men were faring; very few were out. All that I met and talked to had sore throats—all were used up, all complained of being lousy.

Captain Berry said it would be well for us to rest before we went back for the boats and other provisions. Some of the men moved to other houses, and many complained that they had very little to eat—and I was one of the. Frank Berk went to where the boats were and brought back a load. Morelli come from the boats, one of the natives bring his ditty box. Quite a lot of pemican had been saved and we asked to have some issued, but Captain Berry thought best to keep it, in case we had to get away in the boats.

Late in the day some natives that had gone to the boats, returned, and brought some of our stuff. My bag was among the lot; it had been opened and stuff removed; my bed came all right. Mr. Hunt and me had to destroy all the alcohol we saved; the natives thought it whiskey, and had got crazy drunk before any one was aware they found it; one can had been spilled in the snow; the natives ate the snow and, in that way got drunk. Day very cold—storm increasing.

Dec. 4th This morning the natives started out in the storm for our stuff at the boats, but had to return on account of bad weather; some had their faces frozen, but they don't seem to mind it. I called on Morgan—he is getting better. McCarty has a very bad sore throat and a cough; my throat better—feel sore about the lungs. Called on Morrison and Gardner; they are with Shoofly, a young native that was on the ship at the time of the fire; he seems to be well provided with food; I got a good feed here—and needed it. I must climb out of where I am—no food for us, and too much monkey business.

Lloyd went to St. Lawrence Bay village, NUTARIN—the natives there offered to take other white men.

Dec. 5th About daylight, Mr. Waring called to give McCarty his Continued Service ticket, which he found among the things saved from the fire. Morelli came and told me of the house he was at; I went to look at it, and the boy who kept it asked me to come and put with him. I moved over, too, quick, and got a good feed to start in on. The house was quite clean. In it were Ancongua, the mother; Setzmar, a boy about sixteen; Katinow, a girl about twenty; Routinow, a girl of ten years; Waldanow, a girl of five years.

[*Oakland Tribune*] Every time he woke he found himself the object of intense scrutiny from the women inside the inner hut. They could not understand his bearded face. Their husbands had for generations plucked from their faces the hairs of their beards, since facial hair collects and freezes the moisture from each exhaled breath.

House had a good place to walk in outer tent, when it blows or storms too much to go out; inside room is ten feet long, seven feet wide, and five feet high.

Morelli and I had each a mattress, and were allowed to spread them in the best part of the room at night; during the day we folded them up. An old man, named Noad, also lives here; he is a sight—all his body is covered with sores, and he is very lousy. I find as many live here as in the other hut.

Dec. 6th Captain Berry called on all the men at their huts—told us to assemble at his hut at daybreak, and to be dressed up warm as we were to go for the boats. The ice had opened again. We got there before daylight; all responded to the call, as was expected. We made a start; it commenced to blow quite hard—when the sun moves over the snow, somehow it makes it terrible cold. Nearly all the natives of the village came with us; after going about two miles, the storm increasing, Mr. Waring ordered a halt till Captain Berry came up on a dog sled. Many of the men were played out and in no way fit to make this journey; we told Captain Berry so; he said that any of us who thought we were not able to go to the boats, might return—as there was help enough. Six of us returned. My back had been weak from the hurt I got during the fire, my nose was frost bitten; Smith had a toe frozen, others had frost bites on face.

The party went on; the boats were launched and loaded with all the stuff, and, having a fair wind, came to North Head. Mr. Stoney's boat was first—he made a bad job of landing, and his boat was carried away by the current into a rocky, dangerous place. I took a line, got out on a block of ice and, after half an hour's work, we got his boat to where he should have come; the others came straggling in. The natives helped us to pull the boats up on the beach and carry the stuff up on the bank, to a safe place. We had a hard time of it, wading through the deep snow, but, finally, all was safely landed. The ice began to form again, and it was fortunate we got the boats up when we did; at night, very cold. Captain Berry had his wrist frozen, and several of the men were frost bitten on fingers and face—lots of shiny noses; bad writing—too cold.

Dec. 7th At daybreak we went to the beach and, with the help of the natives, hauled up to boats to a safe place on the bank; then we got the dog sleds, and all the provisions and stores were taken up and stored under canvas, in front of Captain Berry's hut. The job kept us busy the greater part of the day and gave us some exercise.

The census of the village was taken—including thirty of us, there were one hundred eight.

During the day, Rainbow and the natives that were at Wrangel Island with us came. I got a shirt made of duck feathers—it was a shiny blue and looked very nice; not very cold to-day; men nearly all well, except throats; we have no medicine for sore throat, so they heal up slowly. The new food acts curious on our men.

These marks were made by native boy to show me his writing; whenever I go to write my log, he calls "paper talk," and wants to write.

Dec. 8th Not very cold this morning; we were ordered to come to Captain Berry's hut, as some of the provisions were to be distributed. Flour, coffee, beans and sugar were given out in proportion to the number of people in a hut.I got an old kerosene can, and made three tin fry-pans—one for Mr. Waring, one for Mr. Stoney, and I kept one; they are good to fry flapjacks; Morelli and I made flapjacks and coffee. I had been eating raw meat, not too fresh—so it was an agreeable surprise to get coffee again.

At night we have to kill the lice on our shirts and drawers before we can sleep; the women help us, and scrape out the nits from the seams of our clothes. It is sickening to watch them, but we are getting used to it.

Dec. 9th Quite a lot of the natives left for the other villages to-day, and we had not sufficient force to pull the boats up on the high bank, as was the intention of Captain Berry. Lloyd and natives came from South Head; quite a lot of strangers came to the village to-day; twelve slept in our little hut—so it was very uncomfortable, but it is the best we can do at present.

It is one of their habits to wash their bodies and all cooking utensils, even the tin and spoons we have to eat from, in urine. I told the old woman not to wash my spoon or tin in urine, so now she cleans them with her tongue.

Dec. 10th Boats hauled up on the bank to-day—all the natives not too lazy gave us a pull; the boats were all turned over, near each other—all masts and oars were put in them, sails were taken to huts, so were rowlocks and all small stuff.

Several natives came from South Head, Akuneen and Seneen; they agreed to take some of the men, they had plenty walrus meat and good houses. Captain Berry, finding now that there is very little food for so many of us, has decided to send some men to other places.

Mare Island. 1880

San Francisco looking northeast, toward San Pablo Bay. 1880

Belvedere (sister ship to the *U. S. S. Rodgers*) in the Arctic ice

Men of the *Belvedere* on a floating ice floe in the Arctic Ocean

Native Housing, East Bay, Siberia

St. Lawrence Bay - Siberia
Native Igloos.

Native Housing, St. Lawrence Bay, Siberia

Jeannette, Vallejo. 1879

Corwin, San Francisco Bay

9. Settling Into the Villages

Dec. 11ᵗʰ At daybreak, the men selected got ready to find new homes; Mr. Zane and Berk to go to South Head, Johansen, Quirk and Mr. Hunt to go to Nutapinmen, where Mr. Lloyd lives—London, Smith, Grace and Bruch to go to Akuneen; Deming to Seneen. Tobacco was distributed to men who use it, one plug each. Setzmar fell through the ice and got hurt; he was on a seal hunt. We are glad the men are gone to other homes—now we may get some food.

Dec. 12ᵗʰ Ice formed in Bay again, and the natives went seal hunting; fine seal caught; the meat was distributed all around among the huts. We had enough to make a big pot of soup—I think it is good, and quite a change from eating walrus at the time.

Dec. 13ᵗʰ Heavy wind, and snow flying all day; I stayed at home, writing up my log from small book and papers that have accumulated.

There has been a dispute about the day of the month—Mr. Waring decides that my date is correct, as I keep a day book.

Dec. 14ᵗʰ White whale came in near shore this morning and drove in large numbers of small fish. The natives catch these fish with nets; I went on the ice to help our boy catch a mess—about six barrels full taken during the day; we had a mess of them cooked for supper. They are larger than the smelt. They are not cleaned, but put in to boil just as they are caught. When thrown out of the net, they soon freeze stiff with the salt water on them; this salt water makes the water that they are boiled in taste quite good, now that we are to be without salt. We were to fry some, but the natives don't like to see fish cut open, these people have a great deal of superstition. We eat a lot of the fish, raw and frozen; I don't like them that way, but hunger decides what we like at the time.

[*Oakland Tribune*] The first and last thing these natives thought of was to eat, eat, eat. Hunger and death from starvation were never very far away, and every impulse was directed toward survival, from the disposal of the dead, their attitude toward the aged and infirm, and even their girl children who would never hunt.

The natives, when eating these fish, first bite off the tails of as many as they can, while there are any on the board; after the tail has been bitten off, the head is pointed out toward the owner, and laid on the board, in front of him; then they eat all the rest of the fish, except the roes. These they lay on the board, and when they have enough roes to make a mess, they boil them and make soup; but all of the fish is eaten. Eating fish don't satisfy the hunger as does walrus meat. Heavy wind during the day and night.

Dec. 15th Heavy wind all day—a big gale. I had to go to Shoofly's house to see Gardner, and the wind was so strong as to take away my breath; only too glad to get back. Begin to feel the need of a wash, but no chance or spare water; and don't like the native bath. Rubbed my body with kerosene oil to kill the lice; it kept them off for a while; my back and legs are in a bad state from scratching.

Dec. 16th At our early meal, 5 A.M., there was some walrus hide, with coarse hair on it like hog bristles; I had to fill up on it or go hungry; I had eaten several times. The weather is now so rough that even the natives don't care to go to the walrus pile for meat. I had eaten several pieces of the hide when I had a piece caught, by the short bristles, in my throat, and could not swallow or vomit it from its place. For a long time I tried to dislodge it; then, at daylight, went out to see the doctor. As usual, he had no medicine or advice. I returned home and tried sugar and snow; then small pieces of ice—no use, though it relieved me some. All day I worked on it; then at 10 P.M. I swallowed some dry beans; they dislodged the thing, and I got relief. No more hairy walrus hide for me; I was hungry, but glad to sleep after my trouble.

Dec. 17th Quite warm to-day; had a long tramp up the mountain while the daylight lasted. In the evening, a native came with a letter from Mr. Putnam; he was on his way to see Captain Berry, and, hearing of the fire, returned to Putnam's Island to stop all trading in things needed, and to prepare the houses for the reception of the Captain and men, if the Captain decides to go there.

At night our hut was crowded with South Head men. I like to have them come, as they bring walrus meat. Plenty of walrus at South Head, and I am going there as soon as I get a good hut. With the crowd of natives and the infernal stink of Morelli's pipe, I am having a foretaste of Hell, and I think I prefer the natives who have no tobacco.

Dec. 18th Pleasant all day. In the morning, when the natives started for Akuneen, part of South Head, Bruch packed up and went with them; the man who took him seems to be well fixed.

Captain Berry and Pete went to St. Lawrence Bay on a tramp; news came that the hull of the ship was to be seen. We had some cooked deer meat to-day, it did smell loud, but it was all there was to eat; I ate quite a lot of it. Stinking deer meat is good, but "poi" is better.

Morelli has the rheumatism and has to keep his bed all day. Our boy went seal hunting; I got him the use of a rifle from Mr. Waring. In cold weather, like we have to-day, it is very hard to write—the paper gets damp, and the ink won't run.

Deer feed makes me sick; had to waste my only box of sardines; to take the taste of stinking deer meat away.

Dec. 19th Katine girl in the hut is making me a pair of deerskin mittens; I lost mine coming here from the wreck. Early this morning, Mr. Waring called on Morelli to inquire about a package of tobacco; Morelli lied out flat about it to Mr. Waring; then, after Mr. Waring had gone, asked me to explain about it. Then, when I had done so, as he wished, he acknowledged the corn [?], and I felt cheap to find I had meddled in the business. The first chance I get, I will get away from where he is; no one else in the ship's company would put up with him as long as I have.

Sunrise at 10 A.M. South Head natives at our hut; four seal caught, so we get a good feed again. Heard that the dogs we left on the spit had starved to death. Out on a tramp three hours to-day; below zero, but don't feel cold if wind don't blow. Captain Berry and Pete returned; no trace of the ship; ice has formed again in St. Lawrence Bay.

Dec. 20th I find this a first class pen from dropping ink, but it is the best I have. Sunrise at 10:20 A.M., set at 1:45 P.M. Good ice; Morgan passed order from Captain Berry for the men not to go on the ice, as the natives were to spear seal, and we would frighten the seal; during the day five seal were caught, one at our hut. It was brought up on a small sled and left in the outer hut; a part of the skin was removed from the nose, and burnt over the fire; then the seal was brought into the room, head first. The women always clean and prepare food; we drank some of the blood. I don't care for it, except when hungry.

In the evening I called on Captain Berry; I found him eating raw frozen fish with the natives. I find the cold goes through our heavy coats like a knife; I often run out to other huts in shirt and drawers—it cools off the lice and makes them let go.

Dec. 21st Went out to see sunrise on the shortest day in the year, but fog and wind kept it from sight. Morelli and I fried seal liver; Schuman and McShane came in and helped us eat it. Dog killed and eaten. Ice was again formed in the Bay, quite hard; it looked as if it would stay this time. Native came from South Head on the ice and, in this way, made the trip in less than two hours. I have a hard time killing lice; they are big fellows, and when they bit make the blood run; they go off like a firecracker.

Heavy wind and drift in afternoon and evening; could not see the sun set.

Dec. 22nd Wind and drift snow; called on Mr. Waring; he took dates, and fixed up log from my notes. At home we had a mess of coffee, and were in want of something vegetable; so ate up the coffee grounds. The youngsters have stolen a lot of our sugar. Read "Squire's Legacy" and put in the day mostly in the house; it isn't pleasant to be out when snow is flying. Quite a lot of natives came to our hut, and at night twelve slept there—or eleven slept; I was awake all night; the next night I see a Maskinka getting ready to put up—I am out for another hut.

Dec. 23rd Gardner, Morrison and McShane called to pass away an hour; I afterwards called on McCarty in hopes to get something to eat, but, like our hut, there was no sign of grub; it was late in the afternoon when I got a dose of walrus hide, and not too much of it either. I must look up another hut or starve.

Dec. 24th Captain Berry and Morgan make a trip to South Head to look for the hull of the "Rodgers" in the ice. Not very cold, and quite a lot of visiting to-day; some of the homesick boys talk of the big feeds the would have if they were at home, and of presents and big red things in the window; but walrus is about all we got to-day, and lucky to get that. I had to take three tablespoonfuls of stinking whale oil. At night ate a young dog. As usual, on Christmas Eve we hang up our stockings, shirts, and pants, and let the lice drop down on us until morning.

Today Waldanow found a new use for my toothbrush; I had to break her from being too free with things in my box.

Dec. 25th Christmas comes once a year in most places; it don't come at all in Kamchatka. In hunting through my stuff this morning, I found a small piece of soap at daylight I went out to get some snow; put it on to melt, and had a wash— the first time since leaving the ship; it hurt me to rub soapy water on my body, as I am all scratched up. The lice are getting too much for me, but, as yet, I haven't found a better place to move to. After breakfast called on Gardner and Morrison; Gardner gave me a new toothbrush. A few days ago Mr. Waring told me he was near out of tobacco; he is a great smoker; I called on him Christmas and gave him all the tobacco I had. I called on McShane, and we got the native maidens to dance the Hulo, Hulo; Katine finished and gave me a pair of mittens. I was out in the afternoon and had my nose and face frozen. Captain Berry and Morgan got back.

Dec. 26th Early this morning Pete came to the hut and gave us two sticks of chocolate, our part of a box after Mr. Hunt got through with it. My face was quite sore all night; the skin has peeled off in some places. Mud pie mixed up for breakfast; I tried it, but don't like it. Sunrise at 10:17 A.M., set at 1:32 P.M.

> We heard from Omlithcot, the deer man; he is to let Captain Berry have a lot of deerskins, in exchange for a Remington rifle and two hundred cartridges. I had to use kerosene again to kill lice; the cure is nearly as bad as the disease. One new dish has been served up; it is the half-digested grass taken out of a deer's stomach when it is killed; this stuff is put on the board in a frozen state; it tastes bitter, but one cannot eat meat and oil all the time. I eat it and try not to think it has been eaten before. O'Leary had to find another hut; starved out where he was.

Dec. 27th Our boy went to hunt seal this morning; I didn't see any signs of raw or cooked meat, so went out to visit the boys, in hopes to get a feed; at 3 P.M. I got my breakfast and made up for what I missed all day. Called on Mr. Waring; I had finished reading my novel, and loaned it to him. Schuman is quite sick; he says he has the scurvy—he has had it before; we have no medicine, but he is allowed to eat pemican. It is not at all times we get food now, as there is a great scarcity in the villages. From what we can hear from those who have gone to other places, this is the poorest place on the coast; the natives are starving themselves to feed us. I have known them, in our hut, to go without food and let Morelli and I have a good feed.

[*U. S. Navy*] "Lieutenant Berry, desiring to carry out the object of the expedition, although his vessel was lost, set out from Saint Lawrence Bay to organize a search of the coast and to communicate the loss of the *Rodgers* to the department, having first made provision for the comfort and safety of those under his command. Master Howard S. Waring was left in charge at Saint Lawrence Bay." –"Arctic Expeditions - The *Jeannette*, the *Rodgers*, and the *Alliance*," from the *Annual Report of the Secretary of the Navy, November 28, 1881—*

Dec. 28th Before daylight this morning, Captain Berry and a native started for Cape Sergkaman; Captain Berry had a team of seven dogs, and is to send or bring us salt, mustard, pepper, tobacco, coffee, sugar, and some deerskin. During the day, Grace and Bruch came from Akuneen; at night they stopped at the Widders

[?] with McShane. I played dominoes with Gardner.

Dr. Castillo says that for fifteen days he has had no operation of the bowels; he took Pete with him and went to Nutapiumen to see Mr. Hunt; the Dr. is looking as he hadn't a friend in the town. Ice good for hunting; day not very cold; new skin on my nose and face.

Dec. 29th Boy went out hunting and caught a big seal; we had a big feed as soon as it could be cooked; quite a lot of visitors came from South Head, and, as usual, had to put up at our hut. Called at Mr. Waring's hut; played casino and dominoes. Heard that Bruch had a good home, and am glad of it; no grub at the hut where McCarty stops; I moved out of that ranch for the same cause. There is scarcely anything else, except weather and poor food, to talk or think about.

Dec. 30th London came at daybreak; we had a good feed of seal meat; we expect to have something to eat for a few days; I invite all the boys to come around about feeding time. Our boarding house is extra good to the white man. Dr. Castillo has returned; he is better; had a wash in the snow. A native came from Putnam's Island; reports a wreck on the coast; Mr. Putnam to investigate. Boy is making a rope from the big sealskin. I had a big tramp; called on Shoofly; he is a good native and a boss shot with a rifle.

Dec. 31st Too many natives at our house again, so I stopped at McShane's hut; got up early and went to hut; after waiting a long while, seeing there was to be no breakfast, I ate up a box of sardines, that I was saving for hard times. Snow fell during the day; all the South Head men go home, and go across the ice. I had a half wash in the snow; then went to call on McCarty; saw the Dr.—he is all right again; during the day Schuman called; he is looking quite bad; says he has the scurvy; he is allowed some lime juice and pemican.

Had nearly three hours' exercise to-day. Esquimaux girls kick and toss foot ball in this kind of weather.

Morelli has had a big dose of rheumatism; to-day his sealskin pants were finished and the pockets put in to reach to the knee; the pants were made from a good sealskin coat; it spoiled the coat, and the pants are no good—about the way he manages all his affairs. I am promised a native-manufactured pipe by Heppy.

The chances are I will watch the old year out and the new year in, if the lice are only half as active as they have been all the time I have been here.

London, in returning over the ice to Akuneen, fell through and was pulled out; he tramped on to his hut.

*** 1882 ***

10. Life Among the Natives at St. Lawrence Bay, Siberian Coast, Russian Province, Asia

Jan. 1ˢᵗ New Year's Day; not very cold; sunrise at 10:17 A.M. before daylight; I got up, run out in the outer part of the hut and washed my face, head, arms and hands in the snow; it hurt, as I am all scratched up; the lice have made a hard-looking sight of my carcase from head to toes—all red from scratching. I go back into the hut. Routinow, the little girl about eleven years old, helps me to catch lice in my shirt and drawers; between sixty and one hundred is about one day's catch; all big fellows. Then have breakfast—walrus meat and blubber, frozen. I dress up warm and go out; the girls are kicking a foot ball and tossing it to each other; when one catches it the rest pile on, and throw themselves in a heap, on top of each other in the snow. They don't mind the cold. I call on McCarty; he is well; then I go to see Morrison and Gardner at Shoofly's house. Gardner is homesick and is sorry he came on this trip; he thinks of the different things he could eat at home.

Too cold to use ink without holding it over the fire. I find that I must, for a time, keep my log with pencil.

Call on McShane; Schuman and Dominick are here; we get the girls to dance Hulo Hulo; they have to dress to do their dancing; they are full of fun, like the Shaker girls that Artemus Ward found.

We all go out and have a tramp up on the mountain. Met a native bringing in a seal. Schuman went home to his hut; he has not been well and says he has the scurvy; he is being doctored for it with pemican having lime juice in it.

The rest of us stay out about three hours; I return to the hut. Setzmar, the boy Morelli and I live with, has gone to South Head for some walrus meat and deerskin; he tries hard to keep us in food.

Our hut is ten feet by seven deep and five feet high; one can't stand up in it. Eight people sleep here on an average; I have slept of tried to sleep when there were fourteen in the room, with an open bucket used by all for a water closet all the long night, from 5:30 P.M. Till 9 A.M.—fifteen hours and a half.

When I returned, Morelli and I opened and ate our last box of sardines. All the men are looking thin. The Doctor is now able to be around again. Morelli got his sealskin coat made over into a pair of pants; the pockets commence low and run to the knee. I am promised a native pipe by Heppy; I gave him a jack-knife, which pleases him greatly. Happy New Year! During the night it rained quite hard.

Jan. 2nd Had some boiled beans this morning; they are good for a change; ate sugar on them; then ate walrus meat raw. This meat is full of blood and, as one chews it, often the blood runs out of the mouth; it looks like a lot of wild animals at a feed, each getting all they can while it lasts, for we hear there is not much food at the village; it is the poorest village along the Bay. Our boy has not got back yet. We had a drizzling rain during the night, and this changed to a heavy snow storm that continued all day.

Mr. DeTracey calls; we play dominoes to pass the time away Had my head shaved to get rid of lice and nits. Had some seal meat and soup at night; Shoofly called; I went naked and had a wash in the snow. It is very refreshing; one feels burning after such a wash, and has to be lively about it.

Mr. Hunt arrived from St. Lawrence Bay; he puts up with Mr. Stoney; turn in at six, then Morelli lights his pipe to help add to the stink of the room. I am now decided to leave this house and find one where I can live alone; I can't let a man smoke in my face long without telling him things he don't want to hear. If I ever have a chance in my Hell, I want some ignorant organ-grinder to sit in front of me; smoke in my face, while he tells me what a fine people the Italians are—how very generous and noble, and how mean a close-fisted the Americans are, or how the Irish and Germans can be in this country, get all the best jobs, and can't play the hand-organ.

Jan. 3rd Rain and sleet all night; up quite early to let them clean up the house; this walrus skin floor is washed with urine about three times a week, and the sides and top about twice a week. After eating raw frozen meat, I dressed and went out a while to get my lungs full of good, pure air; if there is anything that will give us a lasting sickness here, it is not the bad food, but the foul air, breathed over and over by many persons in so small a place—at least fifteen hours, the usual time we sleep. Often at night do I put my head out, under the deerskin curtain, to breathe —sometimes I venture to let in a little pure air; but as the natives are all used to a hot room, and sleeping naked, the cold air entering wakes them up.

I called on some of the men; I am getting tired of this everlasting "I wish it was time to go back!" Most of the men have got tired of this life with the Masinkas; no wonder—nothing to do but lie down on the ground and think; but no good comes of worrying, and five months is not a long time; we have shelter, clothes, and food. If natives can live and keep fat on this food, I am going to live on it for a few months without being always growling.

When I returned Mr. Hunt called; he was going back to Nutapinmen, where he is stopping; he wanted me to lend him something to read. I am the only one who saved any reading matter; I lent him Lalla Rookh—the Captain and the Doctor had just read it—also, one of Frank Leslie's Magazines and some numbers of the Detroit _Free Press_; he was very thankful, and promised to be careful of my book, Lalla Rookh. Afterwards, he called on Doctor Castillo; they made a very humane proposal for the distribution of the food we saved; it was that there was enough to keep the officers, and the sailors could live with the natives on walrus and old fish. Two of the crew, pretending to be asleep, heard all and reported to us; I think they will fare as we do, and others are of my opinion.

Jan 4th Up early this morning; went over behind the hut where Mr. Waring stops to watch for sunrise at 10:08—gaining some already; sunset at 1:40 P.M. During the sunlight, McShane and I took a good tramp up the mountain to look for rabbits; sat upon the top of mountain; had to decide which way to get down, as it was quite steep and the snow hard; if we ever lost foothold we would get to the bottom about two miles off. Finally commenced feeling our way down, then we slid about fifty yards; struck in soft snow; laughed at each other and took another start, driving our heels at each step into the crust of snow; again we slid for a time, then found soft snow about up to our knees, till we came to the bottom of the hill, tired and wet, the snow sticking to our Navy coats; we have not got skin kuckankas yet. No more rabbit hunting for me; right away, after returning, brought home Morrison's rifle and stayed a while with Gardner—just long enough to get some fish. The women of the house gave Morrison a new sealskin pants, made expressly for him; Katino gave Morelli a pair of reindeer-skin socks.

I called on O'Leary; stayed a while; he is getting poor living and shows it; told him to come to our place and fill up any time. Setzmar returned with half a walrus. Quite a lot of bad deer meat, but I eat it frozen, then it don't smell so bad. Mr. Hunt did not get away, as he expected, to-day.

Jan. 5th Mr. Hunt started at daybreak for Nutapinmen; later, Dr. Castillo and DeTracey took a tramp for Seneen. In the afternoon it began to snow; had a heavy

111

wind. Late at night, in the height of a big wind, Mr. Putnam came with several natives; had a big sled loaded with provisions; brought coffee, sugar, pemican, meat, tobacco, books, skin clothes, also an order for Mr. Zane to report in person at the house at Cape Sergkaman, to take charge of house. Also, Mr. Hunt to report, to take the Captain's official report to the Secretary of the Navy; this report was of the loss of the ship by fire and the condition of the men, our chances in this climate and with the people, for getting along.

Very stormy after midnight.

Jan. 6th I went out early, in all the big storm, to see Mr. Putnam; he told me that New Year's Day he had met Captain Berry, within one day's journey of Cape Sergkaman, Putnam's Island; that all the men left in his charge were well. Mr. Gilder was to start for a Telegraph Station in Russia; Peter and some natives were to go with him; he was to report the burning of the ship, and have a relief ship come up for us as early as the season would allow. We are all glad to hear of Mr. Gilder's mission, and hope he will be successful.

Jan 7th Storm all day; I had to stay indoors the last few days; I have been getting a boil under my left armpit and now it gives me some trouble; I have been awake all night; have to hold my arm out from my body; the meat we eat brings these boils on; nearly all the natives in the house have had them since we lived here; they can sleep and let them take their course. Now that Mr. Zane is to go to Putnam's Island, I will go to the house he leaves in South Head as soon as I am able to get away. Natives crowd us all day. Morrison and Gardner called. Storm continues all day.

I have since heard by letter that Mr. Gilder was one day out and his sled broke; he had to return to Putnam's Island for repairs, and met Captain Berry, who was able to give him his account of the fire and official report for the Secretary of the Navy.

Jan. 8th Mr. Putnam tells us we can send mail, so I write to my wife and Mr. Milliken at San Francisco. The boil under my arm gave me such pain that I couldn't stand it any more; I took my razor and cut it open; let out the bad matter, and felt much better.

I have decided to go to South Head as soon as the storm is over; it moderates some, but Mr. Putnam is anxious to start back, so he goes to South Head for Mr. Hunt and Mr. Zane; I sent a letter by Mr. Putnam to Mr. Zane, and have asked him to leave his mattress for me at South Head, and, if possible, arrange it for me to go to Kalkot's house; I hear it is a boss place.

Morrison called and worried away awhile. Storm continued all day and night. I hear the Captain to-day dispatched Mr. Gilder to Washington, with his

112

official report, and he is to telegraph from the first station of our condition.

Jan 9th Grub is getting very scarce here; McCarty and Hodgson are starved out, and are going up to Seneen. Quite cold to-day; a fellow hasn't much choice between the rough weather outside, and the lice and stink in the hut. O'Leary and Berk go over to South Head, where there are lots of walrus.

Setzmar killed another pup, but I hope to get away from such food soon; the meat is tender, and if a person is hungry he can eat it.

Jan 10th Mr. Stoney went out hunting to-day and got some big ducks; I asked him for one and got it; put it in the hut for Rautinow to pick and clean; Morelli and I ate it; quite a change from walrus hide and blubber.

Omlithcot came in with a few small deerskins; he is to bring more at some other time. I packed my bag, and got ready to get away from this village this afternoon. Mr. Putnam and Mr. Zane came and put up at this village all night. I gave Mr. Putnam the mail; Mr. Zane said he made matters all right for me at Kalkot's house, and told me I might have the use of his mattress. Quirk came for provisions, and stayed at our hut all night. Wind all night.

Jan 11th Early in the morning I found a native going to South Head, and he agreed to let me go with him for a shirt and a piece of tobacco. I gave him my bag to tie on his sled, and went to bid the men good-bye; talked with Mr. Zane and bid good-bye to him and Mr. Putnam; they were getting ready to leave for Putnam's Island; I saw nearly all the men before leaving. The wind had gone down some, but it was very cold—about twenty degrees below zero; I felt uncomfortable with the amount of clothes I had on. We had a team of fine small dogs. My bag was quite heavy, filled with rubber clothes, boots, overcoat, and some clothes.

After we got up the first steep hill I didn't notice the cold much, but it had my nose frozen before I had gone one mile; the natives saw it, and told me in time to help it some; when I got too cold on the sled, I would run on ahead of the dogs, but they would soon catch up on me when tired. I got on, and the native had a ride; I must say he walked three miles where I did one, all day. On account of big snowdrifts, we had to take a long trip, through ravines, and up steep hills, and when it came to going down hill, that sled and dogs took us like lightning; it nearly takes the breath away, they go so quick; twice we all tumbled off at the foot of these hills—men, dogs, and sled, all in one heap. When we came to St. Lawrence Bay the wind came up again, and the dogs couldn't see; snow was drifting, and one of us had to go ahead all the time; I didn't know the way, so the "one" was the native. I had all I could do to hang on to the sled and keep from freezing. If I got off the sled, it lightened the load and the dogs made a break; I couldn't hold them back with a rope that was fastened to the sled. It was terrible going across the bay in this wind; my nose began to ache, and my limbs were getting numb. Finally, we got over to Nutapinmen; here I got a drink of water, then started to Yandanghi, or South Head; it is six miles from Nutapinmen, and the way we had to come, twenty-four miles from North Head. The dogs began to show signs of hard travel; their feet were cut up some.

I have had some riding before, but this trip was quite lively. It got very cold the last two miles—I had to tramp to keep from freezing; got to South Head just at dark and was shown to Kalkot's house; all the snow and ice removed from my clothes in the outer tent; I was allowed to go inside.

It is a large room, fourteen feet long, nine deep, six high; one can stand up in it—quite a treat in this country. I got some supper as soon as my clothes were off. Tuccare was doing the honors; he is Kalkot's brother. Kalkot is off to Cape Sergkaman with Mr. Zane. At night I was too tired to sleep; my nose and face had been frost-bitten; seven persons in the tent.

*Jan 12*th Didn't sleep much last night, and long before daybreak folks up.

[*Oakland Tribune*] Cahill was awakened early one morning when a woman fell on top of him, her face badly battered and bleeding. One of the men, asserting his husband's authority over his wife, had called her to him and then kicked her in the face, knocking her backward to fall unconscious onto the Irish sailor.

My nose was all swollen, and the skin is coming off my face and nose; there are spots where it was frostbitten. There is quite a storm outside.

Tuccare had my bag brought in so that he might see if I had anything he wanted; a white shirt and two red handkerchiefs, also two flannel shirts had to be given up; then, as I had two blankets, he said he wanted one; in looking over the box that Mr. Zane used, I found a pack of cards and a cribbage board, also a harmonica. Rested as well as possible during the day.

Putnam's party, that started from North Head when I did, got lost in the snow and stayed out all night in the snow; then, at daybreak, tried to get to Nutapinmen, as there was no food for the dogs at North Head. Late in the night, the first sled turned up from St. Lawrence Bay to the village; Mr. Putnam's dogs lost the road, being quite a way behind the other sled, and did not turn up to the village, but kept on the Bay. Then the ice broke and he could not get back to the mainland; it was a bad night for one to be out, but there was not help for it. He walked about till daylight; the storm then died away, but it was quite cold.

[*U. S. Navy*] "Master Charles F. Putnam, one of the officers of the *Rodgers*, had been placed in command of a shore depot near Cape Serdze, to search the coast. Learning that the vessel was burnt, he set out for Saint Lawrence Bay with provisions. On his return to Cape Serdze, he missed his way while crossing Saint Lawrence Bay in a blinding snow storm, January 10, 1882, and drifted out to sea on an ice-floe. He was seen several days later, and an earnest effort was made to reach him in a canoe, but the attempt failed, because the thin ice cut the boat. Master Waring, on hearing of this disaster, left Ensign George M. Stoney charge at Saint Lawrence Bay, and made a minute search of the coast for a month, but without avail." - The *Jeannette*, the *Rodgers*, and the *Alliance*," from the *Annual Report of the Secretary of the Navy, November 28, 1881*—

Jan. 13th Went out early this forenoon for exercise; not very cold. At 2:30 P.M. A native came and told me there was a man out on the ice, and, from what I could understand by his talk, it was a white man. I dressed and came out and, looking in the direction the man pointed, could see a man with several dogs, walking on a large piece of ice, about one and a half miles from the beach; between the beach and the ice was quite a lot of open water. Some of the natives understand English, and I asked them to launch a canoe and go with me to the man's assistance; they said that the young ice, that was then forming would cut the canoe like a knife. I was certain if a canoe was launched we could help and save the man; but they would not launch a canoe. I wished to let the man on the ice know that he was seen, and tell him we would help him soon; so I took a duckskin shirt I had and tied it on a pole; then went down to the edge of the ice grounded on the beach and waved the signal, and hollered to him that help was coming. The wind was blowing, and toward him, and I knew he heard me and saw my signal. I sent up a kite with notice of help, which he got.

While here, I could see a lead in the ice where a canoe could easily be run to help the man; I returned and told the natives that the ice was so soft they could break it ahead of the canoe; told them Captain Berry would give them boats, powder, knives, or anything they asked if they would save the white man. I then showed them how we landed with a skin canoe the time the ship was on fire; they told me the ice would be hard in the morning, and the man could then walk on shore. No promises could induce them to help me save the man. Berk and O'Leary were off to the walrus pile, about three miles form here; if they were here I could, with their help, save the man. It was not very cold, and I watched the man till dark; about 5 P.M., Berk came to the hut and told me the man on the ice was Mr. Putnam, and he had been out all the night before, having driven on near Nutapinmen. Then the ice broke and he was at sea; I told Berk what I had done— how the natives had refused to help me; no help for it now. We then decided to send word to Nutapinmen, where Mr. Zane and Mr. Hunt were; I wrote, early in the morning to be sent. I went out several times to see if I could do anything to help Mr. Putnam, but could not do anything to help him; it was foggy, and one could not see far; then the natives objected to having me go out.

Jan. 14th At 3 A.M. this morning Tuccare took a note to Nutapinmen; I told in the note what I had done and that Berk, O'Leary and I would all do what we could for Mr. Putnam. Berk thought we could reach him at daylight. I promised Tuccare a piece of tobacco if he would deliver the letter safe at daylight. Berk, O'Leary and I went along the beach and climbed up the mount looking over a big part of the Bay; here we could see ten miles in any direction. We were upon the mount when the sun rose; three natives started with us, but would not go with us up the mount. Could not see anything of Mr. Putnam; Berk then went to Akuneen to tell our men and the natives to be on the lookout for Mr. Putnam. O'Leary and I looked toward Nutapinmen, then returned about noon; it was very cold and we had no skin clothing. O'Leary had his nose frozen while out; my face and nose were wore from the effects of frost-bite coming over here.

I went out again at 1:30, and looked till dark; then Berk returned from Akuneen. He had seen Mr. Putnam, and our men, with the natives, had launched a canoe and tried to reach him, but the ice fast adhered to the canoe, making it impossible to get out now. It was all the time getting colder; Mr. Putnam was seen walking on the ice till dark; he was alive, but he had been a long time without sleep and was going to spend another terrible night on the ice. The natives kept telling us one of their men lived twelve days and nights out there, and they thought Mr. Putnam was all right.

[*Oakland Tribune*] When Putnam was stranded on the ice coming over from the observation hut at Cape Skergkaman, Cahill sought the help of the natives to rescue him before he drifted out to sea. "He's a good man," he said, but they did not think that a good enough reason to risk their lives to save Putnam. "No more good men in California, eh?" they asked. "Why do the white men fuss so much over one life?"

While I was out in the afternoon, Tuccare got back from Nutapinmen; he had given the letter to Mr. Waring, who had come there to look after Mr. Putnam. Mr. Waring sent me word he would be at South Head in the morning. It was very cold at night and commenced to blow.
Mr. Zane, Mr. Hunt, and Kalkot, the native, went on toward Putnam's Island; they thought Mr. Putnam was safe.

Jan. 15th At 9:30 Dr. Castillo and Lloyd came from Nutapinmen; the Doctor came to Kalkot's hut where I stop; I had some beans boiling and we ate them. Dr. Castillo made arrangements with a native to take him on to Akuneen where Mr.

Waring was. It was very stormy at the time, high wind blowing the ice out to sea, and there it would break up. It is impossible for a man situated as Mr. Putnam is to live through this storm. He has a snow house on the ice, so the natives that last saw him say; but now the ice is breaking up and drifting out to sea; all the soft ice near shore is unable to bear the weight of a man. Others may hope for Mr. Putnam's safety, but I now think he must have slept, and will never wake in this life; but in a better life he now answers his Master. Storm continues all night.

Jan. 16th These people have tramps, and one stopped at out hut last night; he thinks himself a singer; he took the Tum-Tum, and for three hours kept up one of the worst noises I ever had to listen to; then he wondered that I was not delighted with it.

I begin to get good food here, and have eaten more in one day here than in four at North Head. Walrus raw and frozen for breakfast; the blood is in it, and one tastes it as it is being chewed up. Then we get some tender meat, walrus or seal—I can't tell yet—and some roots just as they are pulled from the ground. Lloyd calls on me. No news came from the other village about Mr. Putnam; a search is to be made along the coast as soon as the storm is over.

Jan. 17th The storm is going down; light wind now. I called on Songboy and was near questioned to death. When I got back found our hut full of little native devils; while as out, as usual, my bag and things were overhauled. There is one woman here, Umcangua, who can make a Hell for anyone who comes near her; she is a little the dirtiest brute I have met; she wipes her nose runnings down into her mouth, and has many such tricks; I get along well with the others and think when Kalkot comes back she will have to act differently.

I get good soup here, and the lice have nearly all gone; so I sleep quite well.

Jan. 18th Wind gone down; snowstorm continues. I went to Merica's to fix rifle; had quite a job with an old file, but I got the rifle all right. DeTracey and Quirk came from Nutapinmen about noon; I was in Merica's hut at the time, and the report came that the white man was come. I thought at once that Mr. Putnam was found; instead, Mr. DeTracey and Quirk had come from Nutapinmen; had dinner there; it was too stormy to return, so stayed all night; DeTracey explained his position to Tuccare.

Snow during the night; very cold.

Jan. 19th Stormy, and heavy wind; but the day passes quickly; so stormy that the men could not return to Nutapinmen, so stayed all night; storm went down during the night. Before goint to sleep, DeTracey explained the Telephone to

Tuccare. We get up at 4 A.M. for food. Every native that calls must try my spectacles, and put his ear to the watch to hear it tick.

Jan. 20th Storm gone; cloudy; southerly wind, which is quite warm. DeTracey and Quirk go home; Tuccare goes with them to beg tobacco. A man reported that he was going to Putnam's Island; I will send note to Mr. Zane, in charge, telling of the loss of Mr. Putnam. I went over to Akuneen; didn't like the place; returned quite tired; had mamea, a root, to eat, and like it as it is sweet.

In the evening Mr. Waring came; he put up at Kimak's house; I offered him the use of my bed, but, though he liked to come, the native talked him out of it during the argument; he told Mr. Waring he "plenty to tell the Cape Sergkaman;" got off without taking the letter. Kimak and Tuccare gave me their opinion of the way we ought to do; I told them I would do what I thought best, and didn't care for either of their praises; Tuccare got on his ear, and Kimak was mad enough to scalp me. Pete and Dominick came this afternoon from North Head; they slept here; I found a boy to guide them to Akuneen in the morning; sent paper to Bruch. Natives are always ready and willing to carry a letter from our place to other villages, as there is tobacco for them if the letter comes safe.

Jan. 21st Early this morning, in the fog, Pete and Dominick started for Akuneen; Kimak and Songboy notified the natives not to let Mr. Waring have dogs go to Nutapinmen. Kimak said he was going to the deer-man's this morning; I looked for to see him start, but he has no notion of gong, only to keep Mr. Waring from the use of his dogs, so Mr. Waring had to tramp over. Droskin's Boy carried his blanket; he could find no trace of Mr. Putnam down the coast. He went twenty-five miles; the natives had not seen him on the ice. Mr. Waring told me if the ice came back with Mr. Putnam, to offer, in Captain Berry's name, boats, rifles, powder, or anything we had, to the natives to rescue him. The sea ice is drifting in shore again.

Jan. 22nd Kimak sent for me to come to his house; said he had news of Mr. Putnam. I dressed and went up to his hut; found a chief from Indian Head. He told me that Mr. Putnam's dog had come on shore. Mr. Putnam had ten dogs; one of the dogs only, came in. Had berries and paste. Heavy wind in shore all day. Berk and O'Leary got back. I had a wash in the snow; saw natives out naked in the snow, washing.

To-day heard from a native that the natives near Cape Sergkaman were to raid the wood house for whiskey; I believe they will, and have sent word to Mr. Waring that he may notify the men at Putnam's Island to be on their guard, and if necessary, destroy all liquor.

Jan. 23rd Early this morning the natives strangled an old man; his boy was sick, and they think to save the boy's life by giving death to another victim.

Berk and I take rifles and go upon the mountain to look if anything can be seen of Mr. Putnam. Now the ice has come back; have a good look around but can see no trace of him or sled; see the natives in single file, with the dead man on sled, going up the mountain to their burial place. They leave the corpse on a sled till the crows eat out the eyes. then one of the relatives unties the corpse and take off the false runners that have been used on the sled to the corpse to the burial ground. Then the native steals away and slides down on the sled, being careful to turn the corpse so it will not watch him, as they are very superstitious, and think the dead return.

I had a row with a native to-day; he follows me around to feel my clothes, wants my ring, and to see the inside of my watch; is as meddlesome as an old woman. I told him to mind his own business, if he had any. He has been on a whaler and talks some English; he continued to jaw, so I went into the hut to get rid of him. Tuccare wanted to fight him; I told him, "Go ahead, one is as bad as another." So it would be a skunk and rattlesnake fight, and I wouldn't care who won.

Mr. Waring is at Nutapinmen, very tired after his long walk. Had a drink of coffee to-day—no sugar; Uncungus, one of Kalkot's wives, stole all of my sugar and part of my coffee; she is Kalkot's second wife and mother of Sayutoon, who is about eighteen years old. When I find her looking for something to steal from my supplies and scold her, her answer is, "He look see."

Jan. 24th Had bean soup early this morning; went out to Omlitcot's hut; had deer tallow and snow, then frozen blood and roots.

Men came from Cape Sergkaman; hear that several of Mr. Putnam's dogs came on shore since the 15th. One had bell on, and one was shot in the neck. This afternoon Emsinto came from Putnam's Island with letters to Mr. Waring and Dr. Castillo.

At night I ate a mess of stuff that I thought very tender, and noticed it was quite slimy; felt kind of sick after eating; asked what it was. Tuccare said it was young walrus. So it was, but it had never been born. I vomited it up and felt better. Everything goes with the native; the undigested food is taken from the reindeer's stomach and used.

[*Oakland Tribune*] It was clear that these savage people possessed some of the noblest traits. The hunters were stalwart and brave, venturing out over the ice in all weathers to bring home food for the village. Many of them bore the marks of their efforts—the stubs of fingers lost to the cold, the scars and stumps of limbs sacrificed in mortal combat with the polar bear. Despite their desperation to provide enough for themselves to eat, the Tchoutkichi people were very generous toward the shipwrecked sailors with their limited supplies of food. Once when one of the shipwrecked sailors was in danger of losing a foot to frostbite, an Eskimo took the foot onto his own breast and warmed it back to life.

Jan. 25th Light snow falling. Went on the ice to see the natives get seaweed from the Battern; we eat it raw and in soup. Merica tells me that when Captain Barker and crew were wrecked here, they promised, as we now do, to reward those who cared for them, but never gave anything.

I had to go for water; a native girl filled my pail at the spring. Ate some frozen roots and a piece of young dog to-day; dog isn't bad meat. Commenced reading Lalla Rookh again. Turned in early.

Jan. 26th Snow this morning; not much of a day to go out. O'Leary and Berk came; brought a letter from Morrison. We played cards till 3 P.M. When they went to Kimak's hut, the cleanest in the village. Songboy called while O'Leary was here, and told O'Leary that Mr. Waring wanted him to bring the letter to him that came from the wood house. O'Leary's answer was not complimentary to Mr. Waring. Then Kimak called and invited me to his hut; I told him that I would not go to his hut any more; then he got on his ear and abused me. I expect trouble from him yet. Wind and drift snow all night.

Jan. 27th Heavy wind, and snow flying all day. Called on Omlitoot; saw Awangoud crack lice under her teeth till I got sick of it, so came home to exercise in hut; too stormy to look out; came near losing my way on my return. I made a paper whirligig for Omlitoot; Tucarre saw it and raised a fuss; said it would keep the wind going a long time. Storm all night.

[*Oakland Tribune*] One of the stranger native customs was that of having a murderer raise the son of a man he had killed. Tuccare had killed the father of Fleebite, and so had to bring the boy up himself, and when that boy was old enough he would turn on and kill his father's slayer. This was the law of the land. "Bye'n bye me mukee Tuccare," he often said, vowing someday to stick a sharpened walrus bone between the ribs of the man who had raised him.

Jan. 28th We had coffee early this morning; had to stay in on account of storm; eat a piece of stinking deer meat. It was black it was so old; all I could do was to swallow it; it stuck in my throat. Then ate some clay. Not much grub in the hut on account of storm, so we have to eat bad blubber and meat until the weather moderates. It is hard enough to put up with good walrus without change, but some now brought on is very old and smells bad. Eating only enough to keep one alive; it gives terrible dreams; this food isn't fit for men, but no other in sight yet.

Jan. 29th Snow has stopped flying, but road is bad. I think team of dogs will go for fresh meat to the walrus pile, about three miles from here. To-day had clay and vegetables; blubber and hide with some hair on it for breakfast, and not much of it either, with a small piece of bad frozen deer meat. I cooked some coffee in a dirty cook tin; no sugar; Morelli sent a letter; McShane called. Heard Putnam was seen on the ice about thirty miles from here, north, one day.

Jan. 30th Wind and snow all day. Morelli came to me to find him another house; he has the gall to come to me when he gets into trouble; no one wants to put him up. Tuccare goes out and finds a place for him; Morelli promised him a piece of tobacco, but didn't give it. Got a novel to read to-day; it helps to pass the time away. The folks had a piece of old whale meat to-day; it tasted like soap suds, but I ate it. The storm keeps them from going after walrus, so I have to eat what they do or starve; I don't pay for it and have no choice; exercise in hut. Tuccare pulls out all his beard. Mr. Waring goes looking down the coast for Mr. Putnam; he is to search as far as Plover Bay.

Jan. 31st Storm still continues; small fish come; boy and Tuccare freeze their faces getting a mess in the afternoon. It is terrible cold; are not eating scraps after the oil has been boiled out to keep the fire lit. This kind of living has given me the diarrhea bad. In all the storm Kalkot came; he brought a letter for Mr. Waring, and tells me furs, medicine, and food have come from Putnam's Island. All well at wood house; Zane is in charge now.

Feb. 1st Pleasant but quite cold in the morning. I wrote to Mr. Waring at Akuneen, telling him that Kalkot had got back and left a letter for him at North Head; Sayutum went with the letter, but Mr. Waring had started down the coast to look for Mr. Putnam, so did not get the letter. Bruch came and stayed all day and night. Heard of grub being stolen at North Head by the natives.

Captain Berry and Mr. Hunt are to go up the coast and call at a Russian trading post for Peter, the dog driver; the Captain is trading for dogs and using up all the extra money. I heard from Mr. Jones that this was the coldest day during the winter at Putnam's Island—forty degrees below zero. Sunrise at 8:30 A.M.

Feb. 2nd Bruch goes home early this morning. I go with Kalkot to the walrus pile for meat, about three miles from here. Met Quirk; hear that DeTracey, Quirk, Lloyd, McCarty and Johansen have symptoms of scurvy; DeTracey spits up blood and has gone to North Head to see Dr. Castillo. Hodgson is not reported for stealing canvas; he is to return it and be let off. One of the natives at Seneen has a suit of it; Dr. Castillo makes the report; DeTracey is anxious to get Hodgson court-martialed, and he may succeed before the cruise is up.

Feb. 3rd Berk went to North Head. I heard of a native's going from this village to Cape Sergkamen, and I sent word to Mr. Stoney, now in charge, that I would forward any letters he might send. I went for water, then went out on the ice and caught a basketful of fish—about thirty pounds. Nearly all the people in the village turn out to catch fish when there are any; we eat them raw and frozen; they break like a piece of wood.

Toward night O'Leary and McShane called; we played cards.

When I came in from fishing went up on the mountain; when I got back found my nose badly frost-bitten; several of the natives here have faces all sore from frost-bite. One native came that was lost in the snow when coming from Cape Sergkaman with Kalkot; his face looked like one big sore; he had slept out in the snow two nights; no food; lost his dogs and sled.

He had a big feed to-day—fish chowder, walrus, roots, and some bad whale flukes; some of the dishes got up for my special benefit, such as stinking deer blood and roots—I try to eat but now go.

Tuccare and Saytum go to Lerene.

Feb. 4th Berk returned from North Head last night, making more than forty miles in a day on a dog sled; the reason he came back so soon had no food over there and no dog food; he brought me some pens and pencils from Morrison. He got some skins for clothing and, after taking his choice, he gave me three of the roughest skins I ever saw. There were a lot of skins bought for a rifle, and others came from the wood house; it was the intention to give every man a suit of furs, but Mr. Stoney and Dr. Castillo took their pick of the last, made themselves new suits, and threw their old furs into the pile for the men. They are two noble-hearted officers. I hear that men and hogs can stand the cold of an arctic winter better than other animals; I couldn't use the skins and bundled them up to return them; Kalkot took them and said he would give me two good deerskins to make a shirt.

I went fishing awhile, but too cold and nose quite sore; skin coming off; it will be a pretty thing, this nose of mine, when I get back. Berk came and we played casino awhile. Kalkot wants me to go to Akuneen to see a boy baby of his sister, just come to the country. Very cold this afternoon.

Feb. 5th Up early to-day; quite cold. I went fishing and caught half a netful; four seals caught to-day. If it were not for the neighbors we would be out of meat; our boy never gets anything.

The natives are jumping and wrestling, the women kicking football this afternoon. London came to South Head. Tuccare and Sayutum bring some summer seal; it is smelling bad, but the natives eat it with great relish; it is tender and rotten. Berk brought rifle back. I gave McShane salve for boil on little girl, Kailen, at his hut. Find it cold at night lately, so put a deerskin blanket on my bed to lie on; slept much better than usual; think I will continue it while cold weather lasts.

Feb. 6th Tuccare got sight of some big pins I had and wanted some for fish hooks; they are just the thing; three for one perk. Two natives here from East Cape talk English; both have been to San Francisco and Sandwich Islands. Plenty fish and seal caught at the village to-day. Berk came and brought word that Mr. Stoney wanted Kalkot at North Head. East Cape men stay all night and astonish the natives with descriptions of San Francisco.

Feb. 7th Early this morning Kalkot told me to go to North Head with Tuccare; I hitched up dogs in sled—four dogs; put on Kalkot's fur clothing and started at sunrise. By the road we went, it is about twenty-four miles; got there at 2 P.M. It was very cold. There is worse traveling than on dog team; it is very lively going down hill; no brake on sled.

Had a talk with Mr. Stoney and Dr. Castillo about skins for clothing; both of them are well supplied, and didn't like my way of disposing of skins sent to me; they ought to have kept them, and they would if they were any good. It is glorious to ride behind four lively dogs; they don't stop for anything, and the leader is very intelligent; London walked over to North Head for four skins to make clothing. He had a coat that some of the men saved from the ship, belonging to Mr. Stoney; now Mr. Stoney has sent for it. Grace had a coat he saved; it was Dr. Castillo's; the doctor wants it brushed up and sent to him, but he didn't think of saving it. I got food at three houses, and slept at Setzmar's. I got a package of needles and powder that Mr. Zane ordered for Kalkot; one kerosene can for Tuccare; couldn't get any provisions unless I would take all; that I can't do. Dogs run away with sled coming into North Head.

Feb. 8th At North Head; called on Morrison and Gardner for breakfast and got a good one and some coffee. Had to start at sunrise; had a time getting up the hill; Gardner and Morrison and Morgan see us off; have had a big ride over the hills; snowing when we got to St. Lawrence Bay. London walked back. At Nutapinmen called on Quirk and DeTracey; he looks like a broad axe. Met Berk and Morelli going to North Head for provisions. Berk on his return to South Head, carrying all the provisions for this village and Nutapinmen, was overhauled by Droshkin and the rest of the pirates, and all the provisions taken off. Berk was beat, and his team started on; he caught it about a mile from the village. Droshkin tried to make us think that DeTracey ought to issue the provisions as he was above the sailors, and he wouldn't allow provisions to pass his village. Droshkin is the terror of all the native chiefs, and generally has his way. Some day he will be shot.

[*U. S. Navy*] "On the 8th of February Lieutenant Berry left Cape Serdze, accompanied by Ensign Henry J. Hunt. Following the coast to the westward, they heard that the missing whalers *Vigilant* and *Mount Wollaston* had drifted in shore, and that their crews had either died or had deserted the vessels. After a severe journey they arrived at the Russian post of Nishne Kolymsk on the 24th of March. Information was received at this place of the landing of part of the *Jeannette*'s crew at the mouth of the Lena River, and Lieutenant Berry continued his journey until he came upon the traces of Chief-Engineer Melville's search party." - The *Jeannette*, the *Rodgers*, and the *Alliance*," from the *Annual Report of the Secretary of the Navy, November 28, 1881*—

Feb. 9th I called on Berk and had his account of the trouble at Nutapinmen; at once sent word to Mr. Stoney, in charge of North Head. During Mr. Waring's absence, McShane took a tramp to Akuneen to see how the men were. Indianhead man returns and stays at house; he brings a lot of lice with him, as usual for visitors. I went on ice and caught a big netful of fish; Berk and O'Leary went toe Nutapinmen and got their provisions, DeTracey issuing the stuff. Berk had the mustard, pepper and salt on his team; I went over and, with others, got my ration of each. Very cold—below zero. All we have to do is wait for spring and think of eating.

Feb. 10th London came at daybreak; told me he was going for his provisions; I got ready as soon as I could and started with him. It is six miles to Nutapinmen and not the best kind of road, as it has been snowing lately. Storm comes up before we get there and I am sorry I started; DeTracey gives out provisions and meat. Dr. Castillo at Nutapinmen; coming to the house at South Head; he wants to see the men now that they have provisions; he is to stay at Kalkot's. I think it is a terrible tramp—twelve miles for three pounds of flour, two pounds of coffee, and two of sugar. I get the piles from the long walk, and wouldn't make the trip again for money. Dr. Castillo at house on my return; I went out and slept at Omlithcot's house. The Doctor always wants something for nothing; he asked Kalkot for young deerskin, enough to make a shirt and drawers; he has Kalkot's women make them. It is quite a job, and for the skin and trouble he will give half a plug of tobacco. But Kalkot is afraid the Doctor will bet a dose of enlargement of the heart, so refuses to do the job, to the surprise of the Doctor. Then the Doctor asked for some bear skin to make footings, not that he needed them, but he must get something.

Feb. 11th Went with Dr. Castillo to show him Morelli's hut, where he went inside. Called on McShane and saw native doctor cure a boil on a little girl. He painted the girl's face and around the boil; then painted her father's face; then the father lay down and the doctor took a stick with a sling on it, and tried to raise his head, asking questions. The doctor struck the father several times and allowed him to get up; then he put the girl on a deerskin to sleep; the boil came to a head in about nine days, so the cure worked.

Last month an old man was strangled to save the life of his son, who was sick at the time; the boy has been sick ever since, and died to-day.

Big Island man at house; trade pipes with him. Big feed to-day—deer's blood, roots, deer fat. The doctor continues his visit at house, so I go to sleep at Omlithcot's house. Very cold all night; got novel from Morelli; trade for shirt and drawers with Kalkot; when I get the deerskin clothes made it will be too late to wear them.

Feb. 12th This morning Dr. Castillo goes home with a load of walrus he got from Kalkot; took a dog that Kalkot got at Wood house. High wind about noon. McShane went to Nutapinmen for his provision, but found they had been all given out; so he got no ration. Some of the men at Akuneen got no flour. To-day Kalkot took a load of walrus to North Head; he is ever ready to give good meat to our men, and I think he is the most reliable of these natives. McShane was angry on account of going so far and not getting any provisions; he wrote to Mr. Stoney and asked that he receive a ration. Mr. Putnam's ration was given him; he had his nose frost-bitten going after it.

Feb. 13th This morning Grace came from Akuneen; we had quite a long talk; played cards awhile, then had a good feed of walrus; Grace stayed all night. Very cold, and poor traveling.

Feb. 14th Grace went home early this morning. McShane called on me; Mr. Stoney and Morrison came and put up at house; we had coffee; Kalkot got back. I am curing up with salve, Omlithcot's foot. Morrison and I sleep at Omlithcot's hut. I had a letter from Gardner. Big supper—deer's blood, fat and snow, roots, raw fish, walrus and seal meat—the biggest meal since I came here. Mr. Stoney stayed at hut all night; the medicine man gave a performance.

Feb. 15th Mr. Stoney went home; left me orders to send account in letters to him of condition of men at South Head, now that scurvy is breaking out among us; Stoney took a head of walrus. Sent for London and lectured him for having too much gab;

125

then apologized for speaking to him, and gave him the use of his tobacco pouch. Omlithcot's foot nearly well. Morrison went up to Kimak's and got a good feed; wrote for Gardner to come over, at Kimak's request. Mr. Waring got back to Akuneen from Plover Bay; heard no news of Mr. Putnam, so now thinks he is dead. Storm at night; Morrison stayed at our hut. McShane and O'Leary called. Mr. Stoney told Kalkot to borrow dogs, as he would send him to Putnam's Island for food. Eating meat all the time has brought on scurvy, also worms; nearly all the men have the piles from cold weather, and no medicine for treatment.

Feb. 16th Quite cold in the morning. At noon I went out on the ice, fishing; caught a lot of fish. Stayed three hours, got cold, then came in. Morrison stays at house all day and night. I called on McShane for a change of feed; there was a big walrus skin brought into the hut to thaw out and get the blubber of it for oil; we are all out of oil at our hut. The women are at work on my weather coat. It takes two young deerskins to make it; there is lots of work tanning and preparing a deerskin.

Feb. 17th McShane went to North Head; I sent ot Mr. Stoney for a pair of scissors and flannel to make a shirt. Morrison went to Akuneen; wind at the time and quite a storm. After he started I went with Kalkot to the walrus pile for meat. It is very cold; heard Mr. Waring had gone to North Head. It got very cold and stormy in the evening; I walked back and was very tired. It don't take much to use a man up now.

Feb. 18th Storm this morning; wind and drift snow. The big walrus hide that has been in the room thawing out the last few days now begins to stink; I hope it will soon be taken away. Kalkot is to give no more walrus to lazy natives except in trade; it seems as if all of them came to him. Had a mess of coffee—no sugar, but it is quite good; I eat the grounds for vegetables. Kalkot copies his name and tries to write.

[*Oakland Tribune*] Kalkot liked Patrick Cahill so well he decided to adopt him into the family with a formal ceremony. Formal is not perhaps the word Cahill would have used. All the participants except the Irishman were naked and painted up with oils and stains, and danced around him wildly. Then Kalkot put a thong around his wrist, and held a pow wow after which the natives all walked gravely around him in review, and in final acclamation patted him on the back.

Bad weather all day and night; too stormy to go out; exercise in the outer hut.

Feb. 19th Storm still continues; heavy wind. A big walrus head brought in. This is the best part of the walrus when eaten raw and frozen; one can eat about five pounds of it, and one feed does all day. They eat the brains; I tasted them; they have a good taste. The hut is full of visitors to-day; one is all covered with scales, and slept very near me. I think the thing is catching. I went out to fix up Omlithcot's foot; it is improving.

Feb. 20th I went to McShane's hut; had bean and flour soup; we invite each other, and that way, get more of the ration issued. Too cold to be out, so begin work on Navy pantaloons, altering them. In the afternoon read novel Asphodel—I like it and think it first class. Have had piles quite a while and can't go around; nearly all the men are troubled with this disease. Berk took a tramp to Akuneen. I made flour paste, and at night had deer meat with deer tallow mixed; this is a boss dish; must say I have lived high to-day; at night slept ten hours.

Feb. 21st Kalkot and Sayutum go seal hunting. I had some beans. McShane came over to help me out on them. Later we figured up our accounts for the trip. Berk got back; he and O'Leary go off on a foolish tramp to East Cape; Morrison left Akuneen for North Head. Very cold part of the day; night cold, no wind.

[*Oakland Tribune*] Kalkot explained that their way of life was being destroyed by the white-man whalers who came each year. A single whale could keep an entire village supplied with meat and oil for cooking and light for an entire winter. But many ships came, and took many whales. "One time my people thick as seagulls," he said in pidgin English. "No little boy hungree. Killum whale too much. Bye'n'bye Kalkot people mukee."

Feb. 22nd Looked over my relics saved from the fire. Thirty-four years old to-day. Got a new deerskin kuklanka (a storm coat) to-day; it is a nice warm one, but the weather is warm now. Went for a walk. McShane had a coffee racket; I stood in on it. Read Pirate's Book for want of a better; read Asphodel through and liked it. Hear Akuneen men are to come over. Out five hours to-day; quite pleasant.

Feb. 23rd McShane came; it was stormy out, and I made a dose of coffee. I have to use up all of my provisions to keep Umkanga from stealing it; she takes it to her brother's house to eat, and is continually stealing in small quantities. It is not extra cold when the wind doesn't blow, but at all times below zero; the wind blowing off the snow and ice, bites the face or any part of the body exposed. It just makes a fellow feel as if he were sitting on a pincushion.

Feb. 24th Had beans at McShane's house this morning; finished up my telephone and showed the natives how it worked. Ice went out to-day, leaving clear water, as far as one can see. London called; says he heard a native out on the ice found a man's arm; suppose it to be Mr. Putnam's, but Kalkot says he got the story wrong and this happened last season,

Took quite a long tramp and at night found I had the piles again, so must keep still a few days. It is hard to keep in the hut, out of the sun, all the time; these huts are like being in a cellar. Natives are getting boils, scabs, and sore eyes; I have an itch all the time—eating meat does it.

Feb. 25th About 10 McShane and I walked toward Nutapinmen; met Lloyd and Johansen coming on a visit to Yandanghai. Not able to walk very well, but can't stay indoors on account of stink and bad air. Deer man came to house for grub as usual; he got it and went off happy. Had a letter from Dr. Castillo; he wants a piece of blubber, and Kalkot is to go to the pile and get him some. Not extra cold to-day; the old ice is drifting in again. Got another novel, Popinjay. My knees have been getting sore for some time and are now in a bad state. Kalkot told me to use urine on them as the natives do; I did so, and this morning they are worse. The walk irritated them, and I may have to lay by awhile.

Feb. 26th Not the best kind of weather, the wind blowing a gale. Knees are quite bad and breaking out. I went to McShane's, and coming back the wind blew me down several times. My back and my hands and nose frost-bitten.

At night no walrus, but frozen seal meat; it is tender and good. Found man to go to North Head; sent a letter to Dr.; Castillo. Days are getting quite long.

Feb. 27th Very pleasant and warm to-day. I went to spring for water; then McShane and I took a tramp toward Akuneen. We were dressed up in heavy furs; took a rest on a big cake of ice and talked over our chances of getting away from the place in May; Bush came from Akuneen while we were resting and returned with us to the village. The natives had a run to the walrus pile; Tuccare went with them for exercise, but wouldn't go for a pail of water to save his neck.

Feb. 28th Early this morning Grace came; stayed to dinner. Sayutum went to North Head; brought back three novels. The walk yesterday made my knees sore again, so now they are festered and very sore; I have to keep in bed to-day. [These are symptoms of incipient scurvy.] London called and told us he was the only sailor on the "Rodgers" that knew anything. Had a soup made of old deer bones boiled, to-day; it was for my special benefit, and it tasted like dirty dish water; got another piece of raw deer meat and some frozen raw seal for supper; quite sick and can't sleep at night. Another month gone.

March 1st This morning am quite sick; no sleep last night. Kalkot insisted on my washing the sore knees with urine. I did so, and they are poisoned this morning; I can't walk and am very feverish. The soup I drank I had to vomit again. McShane called; we mixed up a dose of sugar and water and heated it. Grace and Brush go to the Head. Pete called, I lent him a novel. Warmed some water and washed the matter and sores off my legs leaving them without any skin; hope to rest tonight. McShane's hut is crowded and he comes here to sleep tonight.

[*Oakland Tribune*] One of the women had gone into labor. She called to her husband. He entered the room of confinement. His face, when he emerged, showed his obvious disgust. She had borne him a daughter. Here in this harsh land, a daughter brought no benefit to the family. Only a son could do that. A girl child was useless. The husband ignored the cries of the mother, tore the child from her arms and loaded the infant girl onto a sled. In another, more prosperous time, the childless women of the village would have followed the procession and claimed the babe for their own. But this was a bad winter, there was not enough food to sustain the villagers and the sailors who had come to stay. No women went up to rescue the child. The husband deposited his child in the snow and turned away. In a few minutes the child was dead.

March 2ⁿᵈ Snow in the A.M. Kalkot and boy go off seal-hunting; as usual, no catch; the natives caught several. New scales on my knees and I can't get up or straighten out my legs; feel better to-day, but have fever and find it hard to keep still, as the lice are troublesome on my sore legs. It is not cold to-day. Seven seals were caught to-day. The natives still think the ship will come early; many of the ships will come as there was a big catch of whale last season.

March 3ʳᵈ Berk and O'Leary have returned from a walk to East Cape; at several villages there was no food. On his return Grace called on Akuneen. Kalkot is to get the use of dogs on an order from Mr. Stoney; he wants to go to Plover Bay. No particular business, just to pass the time and expend the trade stuff that is at North Head. Snow and quite heavy wind. In the afternoon Gardner came; am afraid under present conditions that I cannot use him as well as I would like. O'Leary called to see him. I lent Grace a novel. McShane called. I begin to use kerosene on my sores that are extending up my legs and down to my ankles. We have a way of thinking that we do well if we care fore ourselves; hungry, sick men are all alike. I hear provisions are to be issued on the 10ᵗʰ.

March 4ᵗʰ Snowed all day, but was not very cold. I find that I can dress, and go out with Gardner. While out, Yumkanga gets her head swelted for being so infernally useless and thieving. One of the reasons why I went out was that I did not want to witness the show. When I got back I found my knees had begun to swell; had to bathe them all the rest of the day to keep the pain and swelling down. I sewed my old handkerchief on the knees of my drawers to keep the flannel from rubbing my knees. It was cold in the afternoon. The Esquimo men beat their women and make them mind, but never strike a child for his troubles are all ahead of him like a bear.

11. Scurvy

March 5th Snowed in the A.M. Gardner went out to look at the village, but did not like the people as they yell after a stranger. Mr. Stoney came in the evening and stayed all night. Both my legs are in bad condition and I don't feel like doing anything; very feverish; I lay awake to bathe my knees; would send for Dr. Castillo, but think he would do nothing to help me. These sores are caused by eating bad and uncooked meat. Berk finds fault because Mr. Waring hears of his trip.

March 6th Early this A.M. Mr. Stoney went to Akuneen. My legs are very bad; I can't walk or straighten them out; Gardner would not have them for a year's pay. No medicine; all running sores from above the knees to both feet; I have to continually bathe them to keep down the pain and swelling. These natives growl to see a person use water for anything but cooking. Now they have to bring water, as I am used up, and they don't like it. Half the time the bucket is empty. Umkanga has the deck and gives us stinking meat. Mr. Stoney returned at night. Sleep but little; am losing flesh; weight about 130 pounds now. We are all weary of looking at each other and waiting for a relief of any kind.

March 7th Very stormy. Mr. Stoney can't go home; Gardner and I talk over the ship's ruins and abuse everyone generally. Limped around all day and find that my knees are quite bad; I use seal oil to keep the scales soft. Have no medicine; sleep but little at night. All we think of is our troubles and chance of something to eat. Expect whalers in May, then we can get away.

March 8th Storm goes down. I have no appetite. Mr. Stoney goes home; he is to speak to Dr. Castillo about my sickness; disease is spreading over my legs. Gardner is now getting sick and thinks that I am being used very rough; says he would not stay here at any price. Another one of these damn walrus skins brought in and stinks all night. Umkanga pulled the skin from under us; I fight with her all the time; it reminds me of boy-times to have some one to find fault with. We have no ambition to read and I am too ill to think of any subject long at a time. This part of the Search Expedition wasn't figured in.

March 9th I am quite used up and hungry this A.M. Had to dress up and get out in the outer hut; find that it has been snowing all night; it was terrible to stay in the hut last night with the walrus skin. It is soft now; the blubber on it is quite rotten and I hope it will be removed soon. Old Tuccare insulted Gardner and made him go for water. As usual, all the boys in the village were after him. I made it interesting for Tuccare by telling him if he carried on that way he would fall short at the time of the distribution. I wish that Gardner would go home and I advise him to go, but he finds no means yet of going to North Head. McShane sent me 3 lbs. of flour; it was all he had. I made paste and ate it, feeling no appetite for walrus. At night I am very feverish and sleep but little. I know my disease is scurvy.

March 10th This A.M. Gardner finds a man with a sled who will take him to Nutapinmen; he starts for home. I hear provisions are to be issued at North Head, but I am too sick to go for them; ate paste again this A.M. Am not able to walk. McShane calls on me at night. Some medicine came; I got off all the hard scales, then washed my legs and applied vaseline. I have very little; put lint and bandages on legs; felt better. I had a letter from Dr. Castillo, and he says that he is coming very soon. I slept well at night.

March 11th No appetite this A.M. Walrus is the only food; we got no vegetables this A.M. Ducks were seen off shore, the sign of ice breaking up early, so natives say. McShane is to stay here tonight; his hut is crowded. I am glad as I want his assistance; I have to remove the bandages and lint I put on my legs last night; it was the worst I have found the job yet. I used warm water to soften the scales as the lint had gotten into them; it took lint, scales, and skin off and left a matterated, stinking sore, all raw. The pain nearly made me faint. I washed it until the smell left; rubbed vaseline on and lay down again before my legs stiffened. No supplies; no sleep tonight.

March 12th Storming again this A.M. Morelli starts for North Head. I have to send for Dr. Castillo; sent a note telling him of my condition. Again bathe my sores; if I press my legs with my fingers, the holes remain a long time. The storm drives Morelli back. Berk's dogs came home without him; he brought provisions from North Head and tells me that Dr. Castillo is coming over. I have been feverish all day; sleep but little at night.

March 13th Washed and bandaged up my legs; ate some walrus; slept some this A.M. Provisions are issued; put on some flour and pemican to make a sou; it was quite good. Dr. Castillo came and made an examination and said it was nothing but a little rash, and I must have poisoned it. I must not scratch the sores. He says it is not scurvy but I know better; he doesn't want to tell me. His visit was no use to me. He sleeps at Kuncks. McCarty, Denning and Hodgson came to North Head for food; McCarty and Denning are to stay until all the food is used up at Seeneen.

March 14th Doctor says there are six cases of scurvy among our men; he goes to Akuneen. High wind, and snow flying. I feel some better and dress warm and go out in Yaranga for fresh air, and Morrison and Gardner settle while there. Eat pemican to-day. Very stormy all day; wind and snow tonight. I am to go out all I can, sick or well.

March 15th Snow falling; no wind. I had very little sleep last night, so don't feel well this A.M. Kalkot comes back hungry for a piece of deer meat. Castillo calls on me on his way home; he is to send me a piece of soap. I asked him for a can of preserved meat; there is plenty at North Head. I don't think I will get it. Doctor brings a load of walrus to North Head with 10 dogs, 4 from Kerrick. McShane called. McCarty and Denning are to stay at this village; McCarty lives with Utilli, and Denning with Kanaray.

March 16th Snow and wind this A.M. I got out but can walk although my legs are not improving; big running sores on each knee. McShane called a big part of the day. Our outer hut is a good loafing place and all the native boys assemble there to-day. Kalkot brought a new skin of a deer; on the fleshy side it is full of large ticks and the native boys take them out and eat them. It is disgusting to see them at their feed. I can't stand straight; have a poor appetite and sleep little at night.

March 17th Roots and deer meat for breakfast. Medicine man called in to look at Zemtiners; quite a ceremony. I had to go for water to wash the matter off the only pair of drawers I had. On my return native abused, struck, and knocked me down because I couldn't stand straight. Washed clothes and informed Kalkot that I was not going for any more water while at his house; he did not like it. I have been quite sick all day. At night Hulo Hulo; I got up and went out to another hut to sleep; Kalkot got angry about it.

[*Oakland Tribune*] On St. Patrick's day the Irishman had a fight with the bully Tuccare, but was too weakened by scurvy to defend himself. Seaman Berk came to his defense, and with some skilled wrestling maneuvers

133

overthrew the native not once but twice. The humiliation was more than he could bear. "It's only a matter of time till Tuccare gets me," Cahill said to Dr. Jones, "unless I get him first."

March 18th Came home early. Kalkot was going to North Head with Mr. Stoney's walrus. I answered letters. Sent word to Mr. Waring of my condition and treatment; wrote to Gardner and Morrison. Kalkot got back at night; brought a tablespoon full of vaseline. Mr. Waring would not let me have any fresh meat; rather leave it for the natives one of these days. London is quite sick; swelling on leg. Tobacco and letter from Dr. Castillo.

March 19th Doctor sent me tobacco for London and Morelli; I sent London his. Gardner sent me a note. McShane went to Akuneen. Grace came and had dinner; he stayed at McShane's house all night. My legs are bad again, so I lay on the bed all day. I expect no help from Dr. Castillo; no appetite, so eat no supper. Last night I slept well, the first night for many months.

March 20th London's leg is still badly swollen. I got out early and stayed in Yaranga for about an hour. McShane called and we had a feed. It is not very cold to-day; snow melting; no break in the floe but open water seen from hills. At night news came that Drs. Jones and Peterson came from Wood House to North Head; brought pork and tomatoes out; the two doctors sit on a big piece of skin in the snow. All the crew think I am in bad shape.

March 21st Grace went to North Head. London just able to walk. Peterson starts for Wood House and takes Dr. Castillo. Dr. Jones comes to North Head and puts up at out house. Kalkot sends old Tuccare to Omlithcot's hut but I expect him back at any moment. Doctor, as soon as settled, bandaged up London's leg; all the men call on him. Morrison comes for feed. Native woman dies; big ceremonies at the time of death. Little boy smothered in hut next to us; boys and men count up here.

March 22nd Saw Maskinka's funeral.

[*Oakland Tribune*] Some of the sailors, rambling about in the snow-covered hills, came upon the body of a dead Siberian native and brought it in to the village for a proper burial. The natives were incensed. Cahill heard the disturbance: "Mukee, Kukee!" ("Kill, kill!") A throng of men gathered around the huts where the white men stayed, brandishing spears and knives of bone. It looked as though the shipwrecked sailors were about to be massacred, without knowing why. They gathered to defend themselves with the few weapons that had been salvage from the wreck. "Make every shot count! Get your man!" was the command.

[*Oakland Tribune*] The white men were at a loss as to what had enraged the native Tchoutchis, until the chief Ranaow had calmed his fellows and explained that by bringing the body of the dead man in they had interfered with the native cycle of life and death. They did not believe in burying their dead, but rather brought the bodies to the top of a hill and left them there exposed to be consumed by the birds and wild animals. "Why plantum," he said, pointing to the corpse which had caused the trouble. "Why you plantum. No grow. Me take top hill. Bye'n bye wolf come. Eatum. Then Ranaow catchum nice fat wolf."

Morelli refuses to let the doctor have the use of one of his boxes, and jaws me for asking for it. McCarty and Shuman call on Doctor. Dominick is off on a tramp. Dr. Jones examined my legs; Doctor gave me some biscuits and chocolate; quite a treat. Grace goes to Akuneen; Morrison goes to North Head with food. At night the Doctor said I had scurvy very bad.

March 23rd Stayed in nearly all day. My legs are getting better. Read a novel all day. Storm in the afternoon and evening. Doctor broke out the provisions he brought down; gave me some tea; I made some right away. Boy slept along side of me. Drowsy in the A.M. as usual.

March 24th Kalkot bought a dog "McKinna," 7 lbs. of tobacco, one spoon, and one box of caps. I went out for a few hours. Denning calls for treatment—"stricture." Native puts up at house all night. Kalkot tells us how he killed his father, and how children are born. Sores are breaking out on my arms; now legs are quite well again; only a few running sores. Lice very troublesome.

March 25th Men start for Wood House. Dr. Jones and I send letters to Mr. Zane. Have hard tack for breakfast; Doctor eats pork; gave me some reindeer meat and cake. Natives eat sculpin. Kalkot goes seal hunting. Quarterman "Pete" calls. McCarty sprained his ankle fighting with Kerrick; all men wrestle and box with natives.

March 26th Took a long walk to-day. Dr. Jones gave me a piece of cake, about a teaspoonful Find that Doctor has lots of visitors; he goes to see Kerrick and gets deer meat and berries. Sun rises at 5:35 A.M. Tuccare came back just to keep me awake all night. I work on sun glasses, as the snow blinds us.

March 27th Have a big tramp in the sun to test my spectacles; find on my return that my legs are quite bad again; all broken out. Start a pair of wooden specks. Dr. Jones calls on me to witness that he is receipting for some money, in case that he does not live the trip out; receipt in book. Had no sleep last night.

March 28th Stayed in all day. Grace and Brush called. My legs are quite bad again; have to keep water on them to keep down the swelling; I can't walk. Dr. Jones gave me some vaseline, the only medicine he has. In the afternoon read Jacob Faithful; appetite all right, as I can eat raw walrus. Grub getting short. Gave wooden specks to McShane.

March 29th Kept on my back nearly all day and read. Dr. Jones gave me some coffee in the afternoon. Mr. Waring came and stayed all night. I went out to Omlithcot's hut; no sleep; these people can sleep or eat at all times. Brush, Smith and Rhode called. McCarty is getting better; says we will all die here.

March 30th Deer meat at breakfast at our house; it smelt bad, but Boy had been keeping it for me. I got sick at my stomach and threw it up on leaving the hut. Came to house at 9 A.M. Mr. Waring goes home; leaves knife. Legs quite bad to-day.

March 31st In doors all day; scurvy and fever all day; am trying bath of cold water on sores. London called and got a pack of new cards from Jones. Denning came for medicine; he has moved to Songboy's hut; will stay there about a week. Quite a lot of natives in all day. Sun shining all day.

April 1st Better this A.M. Can stand; am to stay in all day; new skin forming on legs and knees. Lloyd and Johnson called in on way to Akuneen; asked for some food, and by mistake I gave them some dog soup of stinking meat. They ate it all up. Demcenga is to be bounced. Deer men stay all night and sing Hulo Hulo.

April 2nd Legs better, so go out for a walk on the ice; met Morgan and Morrison coming for food. Turned back; we came to the house to eat, then to Akuneen. McCarty has a row with Utilli, and I am called in to settle it; his Irish keeps him in hot water all the time.

April 3rd My legs are improving. I gave Boy tobacco to go for water; new arrangement with Kalkot. I have to wash drawers again; have a tough time wringing them out in the cold; my fingers get frost bitten. Read the novel Bound to the Wheel. Morrison and Morgan came through on their way home. Moving around keeps one from thinking of his troubles.

April 4th Stay in nearly all day to let clothes dry; have to wash all over. I think the biggest part of sickness is over. Doctor gives me some of his provisions. Pete calls. Sore mouth. Smith and Brush have the scurvy; breaking out on legs.

April 5th Went out early; climbed the hill and had an hour's rest on the rock; too late for dinner. Rumcanya's sister dies. House quarantined for five days; now cleaning house. Have to eat old walrus all the time. A piece of soap comes from Morrison.

April 6th Wind from south breaks up ice; snow is flying all day. McShane calls in outer hut; I go and send a letter by him for North Head. Today passes slowly; Doctor wished it was 26th. Rumcanyas cries all the time. Wash in Snow. Kalourigan went for the water.

April 7th Out part of the day. Knees are now in good condition; scars remain and itch. Grace and Pete called; house quarantined; I smuggle medicine to them. I trade for soup for McCarty. Caught 3 seals; I cleaned Doctor's shotgun. Ice is now broken; snow melting; went out walking; expect whalers soon.

April 8th Pleasant all day. McCarty's ankle is better ; Smith has scurvy all over his body. Dr. Jones and I go to Sionigan's to eat duck; Syutin 1 duck; we are not allowed to cook it yet on account of quarantine. Fresh duck is a great change from the old whale and walrus that we have been living on.

April 9th Mourning is nearly over; man reports that the crows have eaten out the eyes of the corpse; the mourners then march around the village. McShane went to Akuneen. Brush and a native have a fight; Brush is going to shoot him. Dr. Jones is quite sick all the time. I fry duck and cook coffee for breakfast. Dr. Jones isn't very ambitions to get back; he thinks that it is all up with us and I often think that he contemplates suicide, so I watch him. We have the ship's money here.

April 10th Have fried duck and hardtack for breakfast; this A.M. got a seal liver from Merica for chocolate and hardtack. I went to McShane's house. Shoofly brought a pair of boots for Dr. Jones. Natives died from fall and wrestling. Dogs crawl slowly now; sick all day. I made seal skin sun specks; overhead box; all hands on the lookout for whalers. Men talk of what they will do when food is plenty.

April 11th Tuccare goes to North Head. I send my letters to Gardner and Morrison; sent Gardner my dress coat. When Tuccare returned, he brought my Pirogans; he wanted lots of praise and a shirt. I went to Heppy's house; got 2 lbs. of deer and some roots. We eat a clay here that tastes good.

April 12th I went out to the walrus pile to help Kalkot get out a skin; dug out three and set up a big tree out of snow. It drifted in; no wood grows on this coast. A big storm up before I got home. Hear London is with a native on the ice, and ice broke from mainland. A canoe is launched, and McShane, Kalkot and natives go after them. I went for natives to carry letter to Mr. Waring. We cooked deer meat and coffee; a first-class feed.

April 13th I hear two natives are on the ice at sea off Akuneen. Snowing, not cold. Mr. Stoney came and put up at Kerrick's; Dr. calls on him. Tuccare stops all night; ice is fast breaking and going to sea; plenty of water for a relief ship to come now. Natives catch quite a lot of ducks. O'Leary calls; I made tea and gave Denning, McCarty and O'Leary each a pair of seal skin sun spectacles.

April 14th Mr. Stoney goes to deer camp. Grace called in on his way to North Head; at night Mr. Stoney returned. Smith called and I gave him some pork and salt. Orders were issued for our men to to go on the ice. Tuccare brings a young walrus flipper.

April 15th Mr. Stoney called and said that Hodgson had traded cartridges for deer meat. London, O'Leary, McShane and Morelli go for our provisions at North Head; returned in the afternoon and the stuff was distributed at Merica's hut. All the natives are in village off North Head. London took Doctor's needles; Grace gave Dr. Jones his tomatoes. I had a feed of hardtack and gave my provisions to Dr. Jones to keep. He cannot eat the stuff that we have gotten used to.

April 16th Early this A.M. I went to walrus pile to get skin, with Sayutim; set up skin to tan, then took sled and dogs and went to Nutapinem to see Quirk and boys; had a good run and ride. Did not sleep at night. Doctor is quite sick and wrote to Mr. Zane to bring provisions. Kalkot is to go in a few days. Lice keep me awake. It snowed all night.

April 17th Home all day; quite cold. Kalkot doesn't start on account of natives bringing in food from walrus pile. He is collecting all his trade stuff; expects 2 dogs, we hear, from Indian Point. Whalers are seen; no ice. Berk and London leave for Plover Bay without orders. Sayutim caught a seal to-day.

April 18th Kalkot starts at daylight; sunrise at 4:45. Doctor and I have seal liver fried. I gave McShane an overcoat; Quirk and Lloyd call and have a feed. Lloyd was beaten the last time he left his village when Droskin returned. Six sleds left for Cape Sergkaman.

April 19th It is cold and snow has been flying all day I have started reading Gibbon's <u>History of the Fall of the Roman Empire</u>. In the afternoon I made dough nuts, using seal oil to fry them in. McShane called and we played cards. Old Tuccare is again on his dig because he gets no coffee; the women think coffee a treat. A native goes through with a letter from John Cornelius to Mr. Waring; reports that ice is forming again. Whalers are off Indian Head.

April 20th Lloyd, Grace, Pete, Smith, McShane and I took a walk toward Akuneen; natives report hearing heavy firing off Indian Head. 2 seals were caught to-day. I ate sculpins. It is quite cold. Sunrise at 4 A.M. I go to bed at 9 P.M. Big talk to-day about relief ship and chance of getting home.

April 21st I read the <u>History</u>. Grace called; Rhode is to make me some shirts. Stormy in the afternoon. Grace goes out to see Tuccare; makes seal spear. 3 seals caught; I trade for a liver to cook pork.

April 22nd Went out for a walk on the ice; met all the men near Akuneen; heard of a ship in Narcus Bay. I had Quirk cut my hair. Natives threaten to knife Denning. Men leave for North Head. Doctor is better to-day. My legs are quite well and I keep out all I can. For a time all hands said that I wouldn't pull through.

April 23rd I have been home all day reading; storm at night. Quirk goes home and not being allowed in, returns to North Head. Natives take a dislike to some of our men and won't allow them in their huts.

April 24th Wind, fog, and snow. McShane calls to talk of the ship's coming, as usual; we got some tom cod from natives. We have a feed of flapjacks to-day; ate bad seal meat at night; all meat is getting bad; greens extra bad. Ate coffee grounds for the taste of vegetables.

April 25th Snow and wind all day; ice has all come in. Boy again gets a duck. I am reading <u>Moths</u>—it is a first class novel. Went to bed at 10 P.M. and I noticed that the Doctor did not sleep well. He is weary of this trip and sorry that he came.

April 26th Heavy south wind; ice is all frozen again. Doctor is quite sick. The itch is breaking out in my old scurvy sores; lice and these sores have kept me busy all winter.

April 27th South wind all day and night; men go for ducks with slings. Daylight at 2:30 A.M.; no sun has been seen for five days; warm wind.

April 28th Natives called me at 5 P.M. to look at a sail and I could see a ship's sail off on the horizon. Watched it awhile; snow and south wind. Whale ship reported at Plover Bay. Grace called; got two ducks. To-day is so warm out, even in one shirt. Umcanga spoils the fire.

12. Rescue

April 29ᵗʰ All men come from Akuneen to look at the ship; we went back with the men to Akuneen. The men feel jubilant at sight of relief. Made out the vessel with opera glasses to be a steamer. We suppose B. Droshkin [a Russian, not one of the *Rodgers* men] sent for ships; the men are talking of going to the vessel.

April 30ᵗʰ No native is willing to go to the ship. It is plainly seen to-day about 10 miles off; lots of loose ice between us. I traded for a duck and had a fry. Read outside; it was not cold; the ice is melting; had a walk on the ice. I have an itch all over my body. McShane goes to Nutapinmen and reports men to have itch and scurvy, and that they are anxious to get away from dirt, lice, and poor food.

May 1ˢᵗ I got out early; it is warm and clear. Can see the whaler. Met Akuneen men on way to North Head. Brush and Smith call on doctor for rags; Smith's arm is bad with scurvy; Brush has sore legs. Wopesooligan and Bruch played the harmonica and ate the duck that I cooked for Dr. Jones. Grace stayed all night; he is not strong and does not know how to care for himself. A man has to always be on the lookout if he wants to hold out.

May 2ⁿᵈ The wind is blowing a gale; the ice went out to sea; cold again. We have had very little sleep since we lost our ship; all the men talk of is their miserable condition, food, and how to get away.

May 3ʳᵈ Storm continues with wind and snow flying. I call on McShane and get my pantaloons; fell on account of weak legs; snow down my back and got rolled over generally; natives had to laugh. Doctor and I played cards; he promises to call on me at Manchester if he gets back. Natives call and eat; old Tuccare invites all the "Beats" that come to town to come here, then asks Doctor and me to give them something. Food is getting scarce again; one meal to-day at 8:30 P.M. As it gets warm we can smell this rotten meat.

May 4ᵗʰ Storm continues; it is the worst one we have had this winter. There is no such thing as going outside; one hut was blown down. Boy, Kalourigan, sleeps at the hut. It is very cold to sleep even with clothes on and furs over us.

May 5ᵗʰ Heavy winds and at times a hurricane; the ice is being driven south. I have not been out for 2 days; melt snow for water. I made the soup too salty to-day. I was sick last night and could not sleep. Tuccare is again playing boss. Provisions are nearly all gone; Mr. Zane had orders to leave the Wood House to-day, weather permitting. Grub is scarce but as it stinks, a little of it does to keep one alive but not ambitious.

May 6ᵗʰ Very stormy all day; all the ice has gone out to sea. The natives said that there are several whalers trading to the south of us; great joy among the boys. One house at North Head was blown down; three natives are sent out to fight the wind and if it doesn't go down soon, an old man is to be killed. That is the way they stop a storm up here. Very hungry to-day; one meal at 9 P.M. Doctor offered me some of his hardtack; he is quite sick and lies down most of the time. He thinks I ought to lie down until my legs are better, but I would rather get out in the light.

May 7ᵗʰ The wind is going down some. I had a row with old Tuccare; he is always trying to make trouble for me. I went out part of the day; played cards with Doctor. "Read some," Tuccare says.

May 8ᵗʰ Got up early and went out for a walk; the storm is over. Nothing to eat until 2 P.M. Mr. Waring came to the hut; played cards and had a meal of raw walrus meat. I had another row with Tuccare; I refused to bring water for him. I went out toward Akuneen and when I returned, Tuccare threw me down and tried to cut my face and bite my nose off. I will go to North Head tomorrow as I am afraid of him. London got back today. Mr. Waring gave him quite a talking to about leaving without orders; Mr. Waring goes to Akuneen. At night I had the Doctor's razor as I had to sleep near Tuccare; if he moved, I intended to kill him if possible.

[*Oakland Tribune*] On this morning, when Cahill was most weakened by scurvy, Kalkot's brother Tuccare made his move to enslave the Irishman once and for all. "You get water," he ordered, pointing to the spring which supplied the village. He answered with a torrent of curses such as only an Irishman can volley forth. Tuccare sprang forward and knocked him down, cutting his face with a stone knife and trying to bite off his nose. He was saved when the seaman Berk came on the scene, but slept that night with a razor in his hand, ready to kill the bully if he was attacked once more. In the morning Cahill left for the village of North Head twenty-four miles away. The man followed him, and would have killed him out in the snow had not another hunting party interrupted the plan.

May 9th Went out early this A.M.; at 2:30 A.M. the sun rose. A ship is seen off Akuneen; I went two miles toward it. Saw Tuccare following me so I returned to the village. I ate some walrus at Amlitkot's hut. I told Doctor that I was going to North Head, 24 miles off. Omlithcot gave me seal skin socks. I started at 6 A.M.; legs in bad condition; all used up when I reached North Head at 6 P.M. Put up at Shoofly's house; had little sleep; no baggage. Mr. Waring would not go to the whaler; does not want to have us packed up until he hears from Captain. Some of the men got on board.

May 10th Early this A.M. teams come from Cape Sergkaman. Captain, Mr. Hunt, and Peter are to go home through Russia. Captain met parties looking for the remains of DeLong's boat crew and joins them. Mr. Gilder sent dispatch of our condition [to the *New York Herald*]; we heard of President Garfield's death. *North Star* brought mail for us; I got three letters and a picture. Capt. Owens sends word to Mr. Waring that he places his ship at our disposal and he is willing to land us at St. Michaels or San Francisco. Now that the party at Cape Sergkaman has returned, Mr. Waring is very desirous to see Capt. Owens.

Peterson and I stop at Aukenger's hut; have coffee and hardtack and dried apples. We talk all night; it stinks so that Peterson can't sleep in the hut; he gets sick. Morrison went to Nutapinmen. All the men from there are on the way to North Head as orders were given to embark from North Head when the ship comes near enough. All seem to think that I am worse off than any of the other men. My legs and arms are a sight but I keep moving all the same.

May 11th Had a feed of coffee, bread and apples with Peterson and Melms got a tin of mutton from the Doctor. Peterson and I are lousy again; some big fellows this time. Heard all the men from North Head, Akuneen and Nutapinmen are on the ship. I am used up yet from my walk. Grace came over to-day from the ship. More mail comes.

May 12th We have expected the ship all day; some of the men here want to start off for her. I am getting a canvas bag made by Peterson. We talk nearly all night; it got foggy. The men agree to start for North Head to the ship tomorrow. Joe Hodgson comes. We stole a can of beef and a tin of pemican and had a feed.

May 13th Grace, Morrison and Hodgson started for the ship at 5 A.M.; bad walking. Men had clean clothes. It snowed after awhile. Reached the ship at 4 P.M. Captain lowered a boat and came through the ice after them. The ship got out of the ice during the night. We had something now to talk of besides our troubles, scurvy and dirt.

[*Oakland Tribune*] On the morning of May 14 Lieutenant Waring had the men all officially transferred to the *North Star,* and transferred the following morning to the *Corwin* for the passage home to San Francisco.

May 14th Very foggy. Heard a steam whistle and know that the ship is out of the ice and coming around for us. Shoofly postponed moving. Ship anchors off North Head at 10 A.M. All the natives come for the trade articles that are to be distributed. The officers give their favorites most of the stuff. Setzmar, a boy who was on the ship at the time of the fire and who had two or three men living with him all winter, got very little, while others that had an officer at their huts got plenty. Men who had no huts got a big share of trade articles. This was like many other of there decisions, and we all had a poor opinion of it. There would have been a different distribution if Capt. Berry had been here.

All the stuff being given out, we made for the ship. Kalkot brought my stuff from his hut where I had left it. He was angry because Tuccare abused me; he gave me two walrus tusks and took my bag out to the ship on a dog sled. I rode out and carried a compass. All the natives come out to the ship.

[*Oakland Tribune*] Kalkot came down to the ship to bid his friend goodbye, and refused to leave, demanding just one thing—a bottle of whiskey. Cahill refused. "You big chief," he said. "You get drunk. Kill people. Then you be sorry. I cannot give you firewater." But the chief had a plan. After an affectionate farewell he had himself bound to the sled and would remain so until the effects of the drink had worn off. Then his dogs would carry him home.

I was invited to the officer's mess; had dinner and got my bag on board. Gave Morrison a pair of rubber boots. On board at 12:15 and got to sea at 8 P.M. At midnight saw a light run up along the side. United States Revenue Cutter *Corwin* was sent up after us. Captain Healy is in charge. Expect they are to take us to San Francisco.

May 15th Captain Healy of the *Corwin* came on board and said that the was sent for us and we were then ordered to get ready to go on board the *Corwin*. Got on at

2 A.M.; bid goodbye to the officers and men of the *North Star*. There was on the *Corwin* the crew of the Barque *Sappho*. She was caught in the ice, cut in two and sank. All hands were saved; all hammocks taken. No medicine, no place to sleep, no blankets or fresh provision. Plenty of liquor and cigars for the officers, and some of them got drunk on short notice.

We ran south and tried to get out of the ice; there was lots of ice and it was hard to get through. I got in Master-in-arms mess; got some vegetables and soft bread and butter; the first that I have had for five and one-half months. I slept 3 hours. 90 men on this little ship; 15 of the *Sappho*'s crew. The men of the whaler are lousy and dirty. We will have a time to find sleeping places. Snow is all around us, and it is very cold.

May 16th We have been running through the ice all day; there is a heavy fog and it is quite cold. I had a long talk with Doctor. Of course he examined us and said that we had scurvy; he had no medicine for it but gave us what he had; he said that it might help us. He burnt the scurvy sores out of Mr. Zane's mouth and mine. We had a good feed; it does not take much to satisfy us now. Some of the men have to sit up while others sleep. Saw 7 sails to-day. Whalers are all around in the ice.

May 17th All day we have been running around in a circle trying to find a lead through the ice; saw land marks, Indian and Western Heads. We picked up a canoe with natives in it. The medicine makes me sick; we have no place to sleep. I get salve for my sores which are on my legs and feet, also a chance to wash the sores; bandage the worst of them. We call in at Unalaska on our way down where I can get some medicine.

May 18th We are still in the ice and running along the shore. Nasty weather; not pleasant to go out. I read part of the day; visit the engineer's department. I complained to Doctor and the first officers of the *Corwin* that our sick men had to sleep on deck and they said it would only be for a few days.

May 19th Ran in shore and spoke to the Schooner *Handy*; the Captain was trading whiskey with the natives. Several of his boats ran inshore with the whiskey when the saw the *Corwin* coming toward them. The Captain of the *Handy* said that he had to go in as his rudder was carried away; he said that they had had rough weather for several days. Grace is very sick. The crew of the *Sappho* are worked hard; have no change of clothing. I think this Captain is a brute.

May 20th I got some medicine from Doctor to-day and the use of the boatswain's bunk, so made out quite well. Scurvy is breaking out on nearly all the men. Pleasant weather. It is a relief to find someone besides our shipmates to talk and ask questions of; we get so tired of one another.

May 21ˢᵗ Storm and rain all night. Men have to lie around where they can. No officer has asked yet how we fared; they are all quite happy in the cabin. We are still in a pack of ice; find an opening at night; run south. We are all glad to get out of the treacherous ice as it can cut a vessel in two like a pair of scissors.

May 22ⁿᵈ Rain all day. Ran close to the Island of St. Paul [largest of the Pribilof Islands in the Bering Sea]; came to anchor; sent an officer and two men to look after seal fisheries; got to sea at dark. We all get around the boiler and engine room to keep warm. I have found an opportunity to get salt water spring baths.

May 23ʳᵈ Storm all day. At 4 P.M. we got to Unalaska [in the Aleutian Islands]; find steamer at St. Paul and *Dora* in Port. We were to go down in this steamer but our Executive makes other arrangements. Captain Healy put the crew out of the *Sappho* on shore here against its will. Natives are dying off fast and the Fur Company wanted men; if they work until September, they will get a passage to Frisco. To-day Captain Healy asked us if we thought he was an officer as we did not salute him; we were ordered to salute. The Fur Company allowed us to get provisions, clothing and pay for them in San Francisco, so we got canned fruit, bread, butter, soap, combs, clothing, boots and such things as were necessary. The officers got drunk.

May 24ᵗʰ We anchored in Port; have to coal up; we are to be taken to Sitka [Alaska] now. I got a trout pole and line and caught some trout; had a big tramp up the mountain. It is quite a city; the Alaska Western Companies have agencies here. To-day I made a fish hook out of a big needle to catch salmon trout in the mountains. Great sport; had a bath; it was very cold but I got off some lice.

May 25ᵗʰ Went on shore and up to the hut; after coming down, went in swimming; snow all around at the time. We get better food now. Scurvy continues; there is no medicine on board for it; that is why I swim and bathe when I get a chance. There is but one industry here and that is the Fur Business.

May 26ᵗʰ Went on shore and got up a fishing party. Caught trout up the stream; there are plenty of trout in these streams. Went on board the steamer at St. Paul; had some papers given me by the engineer. The stores that we are allowed to draw are of great benefit to us; already men are more cheerful and since the men of the *Sappho* were put off, we have a little more room.

May 27ᵗʰ On shore most of the day; went up the mountain to Snow and Mountain

Lakes. At night I am very tired; I find my legs are breaking out with sores again. All the *Rodgers'* men have rash on their bodies from scratching. Took in 30 tons of soft coal and are to sail in the A.M. for Sitka; it is a long ways from here but it is toward home where we are anxious to get at once.

May 28th We got to seat at 5 A.M. and started for Sitka; it is an old Russian-built city. It was pleasant all day; good breeze; all sail set 11 knots. We expect a mail steamer at Sitka to take us to Frisco.

May 29th Steam and sail all day; quite rough in the afternoon; storm at night. This little vessel flies around in a storm and throws one in good shape.

May 30th Very rough all day; some of the men are quite sick and are furnished hammocks. There was a big row with the Master-at-arms on account of grub and smoking. Doctor says that we may get well in Frisco; he can't do anything for us. When I get there, clean clothes, baths and good food will fix me in good shape.

May 31st It has been rough and wet all day; a gale at night. I lay awake in the hammock netting and was sick all night. I am covered with lice again as most of the men are as usual, when it is rough. DeTracey has a headache, of course it isn't sea sickness. During the night forward trysail got loose and stove in windows of the pilot house; big racket. A storm at sea is great if you are on a good ship; there are lots of men on this vessel who cannot stand rough weather and want waiting on.

June 1st Rough all day. There is no place to sit so we have to keep below. Big row in the forecastle with Jenny Legs. We have to run slow against the wind and head seaward. Every man in the forecastle has that tired look that seeing the same thing brings.

June 2nd It is rough, and with our poor accommodations, we are very uncomfortable; there is no place to rest on deck or below. Near land; slowed down at 10 P.M.; saw lights on shore. Places to lie down or even sit down are scarce; this is too small a vessel for so many.

June 3rd Ran into Sitka at 7 A.M.; it is a very nice harbor and well sheltered. Natives come out in canoes (Simash Indians). Expected to meet the Man-of-War *Wachusetts* here but find she is down the coast anchored in front of the wharf. We went ashore at 2 P.M. and returned at 7 P.M. I had a big supper at the Marine Barracks. Fine salmon are caught here; black bass, halibut and cod are plenty here. The natives are sick with fever and pneumonia and many are dying. It doesn't take much to kill the natives;

they haven't much excuse for living as they have no future.

June 4th I went to the Creek Church; saw how the Russians do their religious work. In the evening I went to the Protestant Mission; if all missions are run like this, they do more harm than good. We are to live on shore and room in the club house and take our meals at Karl's restaurant; $1.50 a day for two meals. Expect the passenger steamer the 10th. All the officers live on shore; there seems to be a high time all around.

June 5th Damp weather; stay at the quarters most of the day. Men are cautioned to keep away from the Indian quarters as there are measles and small pox. I still have a sore in my mouth; my legs are quite sore; have to bathe them often; had a Russian steam bath. At night we had eggs and real pie for supper; the pie was good. Picked all the lice off the clothes and turned in to a clean bed; the first since last November. I got some medicine on shore but it is not what I want; am in bad shape all around.

June 6th I looked over the sawmill to-day; it is quite a good one. Took a trip up the beach and went in swimming at Silver River. Met Mr. Rennet. A carpenter is building a boat for trading along the coast; he is an old miner and well informed. Many of the big houses here are built of big logs 30 inches through and 60 to 80 feet long; bullet holes in them show the Indian attacks.

June 7th Kept around the house most of the day; I am getting rested up. There is not much to be seen here. Wrote part of my log to-day up to date. The men get money and have a big spree on beer.

June 8th Get up a party and go off about 10 miles to catch cod and halibut. See miners' camp; catch halibut, cod and young shark; it is a fine place around Sitka. Hear that new diggings have been discovered at Harrisburg, and miners are going there. Everywhere we have been ashore we find or hear of gold diggings.

June 9th Another fishing racket to-day; go on shore and have quite a picnic; land Joe Gardner and Mr. Small. There is a row on the beach. Halibut, black bass and rock cod were caught. Had to pull 10 miles. Tired at night, but if I didn't keep busy, would be thinking of scurvy and scratching to keep awake.

June 10th I haven't been well to-day; had a fever. At night Dr. Jones called and gave me some quinine. Could not sleep. I wish that I were able to do some work; that keeps one from thinking of his troubles. The way that I am now I must have the Doctor again.

June 11th I have been sick all day; it has been raining. I went out for breakfast and then turned in. Dr. Jones called twice during the night; I was very sick; took quinine. There are eight beds in this room and all are occupied tonight. No sleep.

June 12th Dr. called this A.M. I am about the same. Dr. told me to keep in bed; called again at night. I find that I am much better and can sleep; I think he has dosed me with opium; I sweat and it leaves me very weak.

June 13th I felt better and so got up and went to the Russian services and mission to-day. There is no sign of the steamer yet and there is talk of taking us to Ft. Wrangel [in southern Alaska]. Mr. Stoney puts O'Leary in irons at the barracks; both are drunk. Grace sells the dog for beer money and is kept on ship. The sooner this bunch gets away from Sitka, the better for all. I get a Russian bath here, it is a great relief, as every one is lousy.

June 14th Grace comes on shore; brings his new suit and pawns it to buy the dog back; dog is brought to the ship. Men go to the woods every day for a spree; they order a dinner from Karl and do not pay for it; Karl gets angry and finally gets his pay from the Executive. I can get around again.

June 15th Karl tells me how he was put into a coffin to be buried, and wakes up in time to save his life. I make arrangements with Bennett for him to send Catalogue. Issue of provisions to all hands. Dr. Jones gave me a fossil wood curio; I had a big collection of curios before the ship burned. Jones stopped keeping a log as he said that people would not believe it.

June 16th We are to go to Ft. Wrangel. We are on board at 8 P.M. and sail at 10 P.M. While going out of the harbor we saw a light which we supposed to be a passenger steamer. It was the first electric light that I ever saw on a big steamer, and it was lucky for us that they had it or they would have run us down.

June 17th While running through the channel, the ship struck a rock. The vessel leaded considerable; we got toe Ft. Wrangel; launch of the *Wachusetts* came alongside; reported our accident and await orders. Passenger steamer came into port; we hear we are to go to Frisco in the *Corwin* as she has to go there to deck the men. We ask our Executive to allow us to go down on the passenger boat and pay our own expenses. Some potatoes are put on board and we put out to sea for San Francisco. No medicine and a number of sick men, but we can stand it for a few days longer.

June 18th We are inside the passage; it is very fine weather; all sail set. I refuse to pull rope for Captain Healy; he told me to hold and to pull and I told him that wasn't my line.

June 19th Prince Charles Sound; pass Vancouver. Lie on deck at night now; good breeze. 10-1/2 knots. Lousy as usual; we have found that the louse is no respecter of persons as I saw the officers scratch about as often as anyone.

June 20th Flying along as usual; 10-1/2 knots; all sail set. Men refuse to work for Captain Healy; he is too mean to receive help. Our executive asks the men; none are willing to give him any assistance in cleaning up his ship; most of them are weak and half sick.

June 21st Saw sail to-day; it is quite rough but we make a good run; we are getting near Frisco again. Write up my log to-day. Mr. Stoney shot a sheep. I can count 19 men in our quarters who have scurvy. It is an awful disease; loosens the teeth and the jaws ache.

June 22nd We were sailing along the coast; saw quite a lot of vessels; there was a good breeze ever since we left Ft. Wrangel. At night a steamer ran close to us; it had electric lights. Our side light had gone out; all was excitement on board the *Corwin*. This was the second escape from being run into.

June 23rd We arrived at the Heads. At 10 A.M. ran into the Golden Gate and are at Mare Island at 3 P.M. Doctor sent 19 men to the hospital. Peterson has the measles. Three of our men have permission to live on shore. I went over to Vallejo. Bought some clothes, had a bath and hair cut and threw away my lousy clothes. I stopped at the Astor House. I have to report once a day until further orders.

Doctor of the *Independence* sent 19 men with the scurvy to the hospital. Some were in very bad shape. I am allowed to go to San Francisco for treatment. We are all back except Master Putnam. The list of men that shipped for the Atlantic side is made up and we are to report at Brooklyn Navy Yard for honorable discharge. We are going from here via Panama for New York; some of the men prefer to stay here and I don't blame them. I will come back as soon as I get my discharge. We bid goodbye to shipmates and sail for New York via Panama.

This ends the log of the

JEANNETTE SEARCH EXPEDITION.

Capt. Berry's Inland Trip at Wrangel Island, August-September 1881

[From Cahill's log, August 26, 1881—
   "Capt. Berry, Dr. Jones, London, Melms, Becker [actually Dominick Rooker, the wardroom steward] and Petersen were to go inland and travel five days, taking with them ten days' provision, ammunition, and some instruments. . . For the account of Captain Berry's inland trip, I am indebted to Dominick, Booker, and Frank Melms."]

Aug. 27ᵗʰ (First Day) After leaving the ship, we pulled to a good landing place on the beach. The loaded truck was hauled up the bank and we had great difficulty in getting it to the top of the first hill; the ground was soft and often the wheels went into the ruts. It was thought best not to take the truck any farther so a cairn was made of it, and names of the party and N. Y. Herald tacked on the bottom of the sled to better protect it. Here was found a beaver worm which Dr. Jones preserved. We then traveled about 2 hours to a good camping place; here Capt. Berry found a big mammoth tusk which was afterward taken to the ship. We put up the tent, gathered moss, built a fire, had supper and turned in.

   Elevated land all around; this our first camp we called "Shepard's Run."

Aug. 28ᵗʰ (Second Day.) With moss we built a fire, and while breakfast was being prepared, Capt. Berry shot a beautiful plover; Dr. Jones prepared the skin and put it in a safe place, intending to get it on the return of the party, but we did not come back that way so it was left in its hiding place. It was a good day for traveling, clear and not very cold. We started and having gone a few miles, Capt. Berry found a large mammoth tooth and brought it to the ship. Made good headway until 12 noon, then stopped for lunch: coffee, sardines, and ham. Then started again and kept on, carrying each a heavy load until dark. Put up tent, gathered moss; lit a fire; had supper and turned in, tired and sleepy. Camp Cataract Run.

Aug. 29th Dirty and drizzling this morning; had breakfast, packed the tent and stuff; each took his load and we again started, keeping as much as we could on the elevated ground. Capt. Berry tried to make for the center of the land as near as he could direct his course. We lunched at noon; started again and came to a deep valley. It was necessary to cross it to reach the mountains beyond. The bedding and tent were tied together and rolled down; the rest of our goods and provisions we carried down, and a very serious thing it was, but fortunately all were landed in safety. After a rest, we started in search of a good camp ground. We found one near a small stream about a mile further on; here we put up the tent. We could always find dry moss enough to start a good fire with; enough was gathered for the morning fire; we had a good supper. All around us were high mountains. As yet we had met with no signs of human habitation; we had seen fox and bear tracks; skeletons of small animals were also found.

We had a good night's sleep. Getting very cold.

Aug. 29th (Fourth Day) We were up at daybreak. Clear and quite cold this morning; a fire was lit and breakfast prepared. After breakfast we packed up and started; we had to change our course, and went south. This morning we fired at a lot of geese, but did not hit any of them; at noon we had lunch and a rest; again started, and kept on till near twilight. A small stream was seen ahead; we went on till we reached it. The tent was put up, and we had supper; then we turned in very tired. We carried with us a tent and poles, bedding and sleeping bag, provisions, rifle, shotgun, cartridges, extra boots, clothes, alcohol, lime juice, and a few things such as knives, ropes tobacco, etc., and instruments for surveying, of which we had to be extra careful. It is hard enough to travel on, day after day, without the load we found necessary to take in this new land.

Aug. 30th (Fifth Day) Up early this morning; had a hurried breakfast, and packed up. The highest mountains we had yet seen were now within three miles of where we had our camp.. The weather cold, but splendid for traveling with a back load. Captain Berry told us he was the ascend the highest mountain in sight, and have London and Booker go with him. Dr. Jones and Petersen were to go up another mountain; Melms is to guard the provisions and tent. At 10 A.M. the Captain and men had reached the base of the mountain, and at 1:45 were on the top. Captain Berry thinks the elevation is, at least, five thousand feet. Here is had a good view of the surrounding country; it was seen that Wrangel Land so called was an island. [This is the first knowledge of the insularity of Wrangel Island.]

Captain Berry now determined to return to the ship, fully satisfied with his inland trip. Dr. Jones and Petersen, also, had a good view, and were satisfied about this being a large island. All returned to camp, had supper, and turned in. Dr. Jones and Booker began to have sore feet.

Aug. 31ˢᵗ (Sixth Day) It snowed during the night, which made it very disagreeable at starting. Captain Berry decided the best way to return, and, after a hearty breakfast, we packed things and started, following the river called Chaplain River. The wind kept increasing, so we kept on until 4 P.M., when it was too rough to go any further. We had great trouble in securing the tent n account of the high wind, but we finally got things secure; had dinner and supper together, and turned in for a much needed sleep.

Sept. 1ˢᵗ (Seventh Day) Clear and cold weather at daybreak; a fire was lit and breakfast prepared. After breakfast, before starting, Dominick tried to put up a job on Melms and Petersen: he put a can of tomatoes in the hot ashes, intending to have them look for it about the time it was ready to explode, but before he had called their attention to it, a loud report was heard, and it sent its contents all over him. This turned the joke on himself and furnished amusement for the rest of the day. During the day Captain Berry killed snipe and plover. After a long tramp Dr. Jones and Becker found their feet were blistering. The tent was put up, moss gathered, a fire lit, and some of the birds cooked; we had a very good supper, then turned in for a good sleep.

Sept. 2ⁿᵈ (Eighth Day) Had very bad weather at starting this morning. We now changed our course and went east as, in following this river, we had gone a long way from the direct course to the ship. At noon stopped for rest and refreshment; again started our journey. Jones and Booker began to lag behind; the Captain told Melms to stay with Dr. Jones, and Peterson with Dominick, while he and London kept on in advance; thus the party got separated. At 2:30 P.M. came in sight of the ship; it cheered the drooping spirits of the party, and, keeping the ship in view, we kept on. A heavy snow-storm commenced and, somehow, we lost sight of each other. Captain Berry and London, just about dark, came suddenly within shooting range of a bear and cub, which they thought were lying for them. London fired at the big bear; it did not move. Then, on going nearer, saw footprints of the man who had killed them; they were shot by DeTracey, acting carpenter of the *Rodgers*.

    The Captain and London kept on; they reached the spit and walked to where the ship lay. A boat was lowered, and they were soon on board, entirely used up. Captain Berry at once sent Hodgson with some seamen up the spit, where he supposed the men were. Hodgson had not returned at midnight.

    Dr. Jones and Melms kept on for a while, after losing sight of the Captain and the other men; then Dr. Jones, with his feet blistered and cold, decided to camp for the night, as the snow-storm was increasing. Melms found a good place under a bluff, on the snow. The tent was put up and bedding put down; the

Doctor's boots were taken off and his feet attended to. They had enough provisions for a good lunch; having eaten enough they turned in, little thinking of the trouble we were having on board on their account. We thought they had got lost in the snow or that the bears, that were so numerous at that time, had attacked and destroyed them.

Petersen and Rooker wandered around for a while; Petersen had found a mammoth tusk and had carried it a long time, in addition to his load. At last they concluded that the best thing they could do was to rest till daylight; so they lay down in the snow; both were soon asleep. Booker thinks he heard his name called after he lay down, but the wind and snow made him keep his ears covered up, and again he slept. Meanwhile, Hodgson and the party sent to look for the missing ones hunted in vain. They called their names, but no answer—they feared the men were lost or frozen.

Sept. 3rd (Ninth Day) About two this morning, the search party calling out "Dominick," heard the report of a rifle and a revolver nearby, and, following to where the sound came from, they found Dominick sitting up in the snow. Peterson was laying on his stomach with his head under a deerskin robe, or kuchanka, as the natives call this garment. The men were benumbed and, even after they had been made to walk toward the ship, could give no account of how they came there or of the Dr. or Melms. They acted and spoke like men who had lost all reason. Hodgson had left the dinghy at a point about two miles from the ship. It was hauled up on the beach and anchored, as they found it almost impossible to proceed with the boat against the wind. It was very cold at the time, and the party thought, as the Captain and men had come near the spit together, that perhaps the men would be found on the spit. It was thought best, seeing the condition of the two men found, to bring them to she ship. They were helped to the place where the boat lay, put in, and pulled to the ship, then taken on board. Arriving at 4 A.M., Hodgson reported that he had done all he could to find the men, but had only seen the two; Captain Berry thought he might have continued his search till he did find the other men. Ensign Stoney was ordered to take the same party and search for the men; the men got on dry clothes and got into the boat.

Deming did not go the second time; a few days after, when Captain Berry came on deck, he sent for him to find out the reason why and gave him a severe lecture. He told the Captain that while he was changing his clothes the boat went off and left him.

Mr. Stoney went up the Bay with the search party; looked on shore and on the spit, but could not find any trace. They landed at the head of the Bay, and searched for several miles along the coat; then they returned, giving up the search, the party cold, wet, hungry, and tired.

I had the day's duty and, as orders were passed to fire up on the donkey boiler, to heat up the ship, at three in the morning I started fires. After daylight often went on deck and looked for the boat; at 10:30 A.M. I looked to the mainland and could see two men. Reported to Master Putnam; he looked thought the spy-glass and saw they were Dr. Jones and Melms. A boat was lowered and sent in for them, and they were soon on board. The Doctor had all he wanted of Wrangle Island, but Melms, who had traveled many hundred miles in the Arctic with Lieut. Schwatzka, looked quite fresh after carrying a double load.

Morrison and I were then ordered on shore, to go up the spit and notify the search party that the men had come on board. It was very stormy at the time; we dressed up warm; after a lot of trouble were landed on the spit. The heavy wind drove the waves far in on the beach, and there was snow in drifts all the way; we had to travel lively to keep warm. After going about three miles up the spit we met the boat returning. We had on rubber boots, and when the boat came in shore we got in and helped pull to the ship; the men were wet through. We had taken with us a bottle of Bitters; it was passed around and seemed to do some good.

At 3 P.M. all hands were on board and the boats hauled up; the men were tired, but all were satisfied with the safe return of the inland party. Captain Berry was all right after a good night's rest—he can stand a big lot of hard usage. Dr, Jones was all right in a week; Dominick came around for duty in four days; Petersen was able to go after his tuck the next day; Melms was ready to start again, if wanted, at any time.

For the account of Captain Berry's inland trip, I am indebted to Dominick Rooker, and Frank Melms.

Captain Berry thinks the island has not been inhabited; no signs of human beings found.

APPENDIX TWO:

Mr. Waring's Trip Sailing East, Wrangel Island August-September 1881

[From Cahill's log, August 26, 1881—
"Master Waring, Dr. Castillo, Bruch, Berk, Grace, Huebner and McCarty were to sail along the coast (in a good whale-boat, for five days), make landings, look for cairns or signs of inhabitants. . . .For this account of the trip I am indebted to Frank Berk and Julius Huebner."]

Aug. 27th (First Day) Leaving the ship, we were cheered by those remaining and gave and answering cheer for the *Rodgers* in return, and sailed along the coast until about 7 P.M. Then seeing a good place for camp, we landed and hauled up the boat. The tent was put up, wood gathered, and a fire lighted; while supper was cooking, some of the men went shooting; found only sea gulls to fire at. They returned and had a good supper, and turned in. No watch stood. Put up a signal red flag on a pole and date with account of Trip.

Aug. 28th (Second Day) Broke camp early this morning. Before leaving one of the gulls killed last night was nailed to a pole which we stood up in the sand. After the boat was loaded, we put to sea; sailing awhile we saw an American flag hoisted in shore on a hill. We landed to examine it, and found a bottle with a paper stating the U. S. Revenue Cutter *Corwin*, Capt. Hooper and men had landed here the 19th of August. On the second cliff North from the Flag, a cask of canned provisions was buried. We made no search for the provisions; left a paper in a bottle and went to sea again; called this place Skeleton Run. Found whale and walrus skeleton. Here we saw in the ground a beautiful mammoth tusk, and tried to get it, but the ground around it was frozen too hard, so we had to leave it, hoping to get it at some future time. Later we went on shore for dinner; put to sea again. Never evening we met heavy ice fast coming in shore. We got by it, and sailed around the Northeast corner of Wrangel Island. We saw a polar bear on shore, too far to shoot it.

We had quite a lot of trouble getting in shore fore camp; the heavy ice from the North being fast driven in with wind and tide, but we finally got safely in and the boat hauled up. Here we found a lot of driftwood, and the men made a big bonfire at night. We had supper and turned in; dragged boat 500 yards to camp.

Aug. 29th (Third Day) The ice had piled in on shore, so that we could not go to sea today; we watched the currents, and found the tide run 6 hrs. each way. We saw a great many seals during our stay. Mr. Waring and Dr. Castillo went hunting and shot some plover, and we had the birds for supper. Turned in early and had a good sleep. Saw a bear on the ice today, not near enough to shoot. Clear water, but Mr. Waring and Doctor had not returned. No making up last day.

Aug. 30th (Fourth Day) The ice still prevents us from getting the boat off. Shooting plover and gulls; also put up a pail with the names of the party, and the object of the search. Hope to get away from here soon.

Aug. 31st To-day a fox was seen on shore; Mr. Waring and the Doctor were landed to hunt. We had pulled up the bay now called Snipes' Bay. Went on shore; had a dinner of snipes, that were found in great numbers here. The surface of the water was covered with them for miles, and they were not afraid of us, having been, up to this time, undisturbed by hunters. After dinner we got to sea again. Toward evening we met lots of ice, that was drifting in shore. We landed the boat safely, put up the tent and, while supper was cooking, we went along the coast about six miles. Found a long sand spit running northwest; had great trouble in landing— only one clear passage to get in shore. Five minutes after landing the ice locked us in; the boat could not be gotten off; so it was decided to make a trip up the sand spit.

Sept. 1st Bruch, Berk and Huebner went up the sand spit about fifteen miles; found another fine specimen of mammoth tusk in good state of preservation. They had not brought with them any tools for digging it up. Three shots from the Remington rifled, fired at one spot, failed to make a dent in it—the ivory was so hard.

Here the men saw the first of the land on the spit and the coast on the opposite beach, running north northwest. Mr. Waring and the other men also made a trip, and all came to the conclusion that this land was a large island.

The ice kept coming in, leaving very little show for us to get the boat off; so again we camped and turned in. To-day we saw a big polar bear and fired at him, but did not hit him. Took bearings of ice; found it aground solid.

Sept. 2nd (Seventh Day) The ice has not cleared, but is accumulating, and at present we cannot get the boat off. All hands had a talk over the matter, and it is decided to start in the morning overland for the ship. The boat was turned over; all the provisions that we were to leave, with sleeping bags, clothing and boat gear carefully stowed under the boat. The mast was put up; a bottle with paper placed in it, having names of men and object of search was fastened to the mast. A bag was nailed to mast for a signal. All was put in readiness to make an early start across the land, for the ship. Then we had supper and turned in.

Sept. 3rd (Eighth Day) Broke camp very early; had breakfast and stored the remaining stuff under the boat and tent, and at five o'clock started for the ship. It was snowing at the time, and the snow kept up all day.

We carried chronometer, sextant, compass, rifles, cartridges, books, a few provisions, necessary clothing, and Grace carried a dog that he had taken on the trip with him. The course having been decided, the men kept in a sort of Indian file, Frank Berk and Bruch taking the lead. Mr. Waring, Huebner and McCarty next; then came Grace and his dog; the Dr. Castillo, who kept the party all day waiting for him to catch up. He was a poor man to send on a tramp; his feet gave out, and he lost all courage.

It was thought that, by taking a short cut across the place, the party could camp at the first camp out from the ship. Toward night the snow turned to rain and sleet, making traveling very hard; soft mud in many places, keeping the feet of all the men wet and cold. At 4 P.M., had lunch; at 10 P.M. the men, to keep from the bad walking inland, had neared the mountain where the ground was hard. Here, on the steep side of the mountain, the men had lunch, and slept for a few hour. The rain a sleet wet their fur clothing through, making it very heavy and uncomfortable. They were very tired, having made a long march, and hoped the next night would find them on board the ship. Dr. Castillo's feet were blistered.

Sept. 4th (Ninth Day) Early this morning the order was given to start; without any breakfast, we tramped over the ills till, at 10 A.M., we came to our first camp ground. Here a fire was lighted; we had quite a good breakfast and a little rest; then we started again and, at about 2:30, saw men from the ship; they had come out to skin the bear and cub that Mr. DeTracey had shot. Afterwards we straggled on to where the boat was anchored. When the bears had been skinned, I had, with a native, taken the cub's skin and hind quarters, and we were starting for the boat. Looking over the hills, we saw a man. I dropped my load and proposed to go to his assistance, thinking, if it was one of our men, he had carried his load far enough. Petersen followed; soon we met Berk and Bruch; then Huebner and McCarty next, who told us the Doctor was all used up and needed help. Mr. Waring passed us next; after a while we came up to the Doctor; then came Grace and his dog.

I took the doctor's big "Kuchanka"—with rain in it, it weighed about forty pounds. I let him put on my coat—it was dry and light; London took part of his load. Then we heard we were not the first to land on Wrangel Island.

The Doctor had to mover very slow; when he came to the river, London and I carried him over, cradle fashion, in our arms, the water running fast and our boots full of it. We carried him over three big streams; then came to good walking on the snow. We were last to reach the boat, which was then anchored at the head of the spit, saving a long walk of five miles. We all pulled a cheerful streak, and, at 5:20 reached the ship. The Doctor used three pairs of boots on his journey.

Now we only waited to welcome back Mr. Hunt's party; then go to look for the *Jeannette*.

For this account of the trip I am indebted to Frank Berk and Julius Huebner.

APPENDIX THREE:

Ensign Hunt's Trip Sailing West on the Coast of Wrangel Island 1881, August-September 1881

[From Cahill's log, August 26, 1881—
"Ensign Hunt, Chief Zane, O'Leary, Quirk, Lloyd, McKane and Johansen were to sail in an opposite direction from the Waring party, and also to look for cairns or inhabitants; both crews in good whale-boats were to sail five days, then return. . . . .I am indebted to Edward O'Leary, First-class Fireman, and others of the party for their account of Mr. Hunt's trip."]

Aug. 27ᵗʰ (First Day) We were the first of three parties selected to make the different surveys, and got away at half past three P.M. We got a hearty cheer leaving the ship, and an old boot was thrown after us by Mr. Stoney. At ten miles from the ship, seeing a good place for camp and night coming on, we landed; discharged the cargo, then hauled the load up high and dry. Some of the men put up the tent while others gathered and prepared wood; a fire was lit and supper cooked. Skin clothing was then served out, after which we turned in; each standing watch in turn, and melting snow for drinking and cooking with. Cold weather but expect to get used to it.

Aug. 28ᵗʰ (Second Day) Up early this morning cooking. Messrs. Zane and Hunt took the shot guns and went hunting. Saw some geese in a pond; as the men came near they flew away. A large flock overhead at the time made an attempt to land. They fired and killed two geese and afterwards a duck. While they were away, breakfast was cooked and a signal ple prepared to erect. On their return we had breakfast, put up the signal pole, called the place Goose Camp, then loaded and launched the boat and put to sea.

A mile or so further on we met some ducks, fired and got a few of them. Three miles farther on Mr. Hunt thought he saw a cairn on shore. The boat was

161

backed and Mr. Hunt went to where the suppose cairn was. He got very near to it, when to his surprise instead of a cairn, a big polar bear raised his head to see what was wanted. Mr. Hunt remembered something he left in the boat, and made the best time on Wrangel Island ever known. When he reached the boat he told of the big bear, took a rifle; all hands followed, some with rifles leaving the boat to the mercy of the sea. It was drifting out with its load when one of the men went back and secured it. The men with rifles kept banging away at the bear while he was making down hill for the water. Then the bear, for the first time, was hit, either by McShane or Johansen, both having fired at the same time. The bear again made for the shore where he fell; Johansen gave him another shot which finished him; then the body was cut up and hacked to pieces. Some of the men drank the blood yet warm. He was skinned; the skin was so heavy that it took four men to carry it to the boat. The tenderloins, heart, liver, and tongue were carried to the boat for food; some of the rest of the men thinking the carcass good eating proposed to bury it until the boat would return.

Mr. Hunt said he would not return this way, so confident was he that he would sail around the Island. It being time for the observation, Mr. Hunt now asked Mr. Zane the time of day. Mr. Zane says, "You got my watch." Hunt said, "O yes! I put it in my jacket in the boat." One of the men looked in said jacket but found no watch; in one of the jackets a big hole was found; the boat was then searched but no watch found. Mr. Hunt then said the coxswain had the jacket over his shoulders and the watch must have fallen overboard. Finally it was agreed the Messrs. Hunt and Zane would go to the place where Mr. Hunt first saw the bear, just before he jumped and started for the boat. Arriving here they found watch and chain; returned to the boat happy.

The boat then put to sea again; it was past noon, the men quite hungry— but no sigh of dinner yet. About two miles further on, the men, with shotgun, commenced to fire at young geese, that were here in great numbers; they were so young that their wings had not grown. They swam to the shore; we followed. The men caught more than the officers killed with two breech loading, double-barreled shotguns. A fire was lighted and some of the bear tenderloin was cooked —the toughest meat ever eaten. After dinner we started to sea again, this time pulling and taking soundings. We saw several places where rivers had been running, found a spring of water running. Afterwards we got a good breeze eastward; put to sea, and kept on sounding till dark. Then we were quite a long way from land—Mr. Zane thought about nine miles; we couldn't see even the largest cairn at dark. Most of the men went to sleep; Mr. Hunt steering all the time. We made for the land as fast as the wind would carry us; some of the men were kept awake.

By the time we got in shore, we had come from sea at least twelve miles. We found a very heavy swell on at the time, and had great trouble in landing;

those who didn't have rubber boots got their feet wet. After a while the boat was landed and the cargo removed; then the boat was hauled far up on land. The tent was pitched, and a fire lighted. Bear meat and coffee for supper—it was then 2:20 A.M.—if we could call it supper at that time.

Here we found plenty of fresh water for cooking; we did not stop to wash the dishes at this time. Mr. Hunt gave orders to the men who had the morning watch to call all hands at 7 A.M. He had the prayers of the sailors. He had quite a time figuring out where he was at noon, and used up the next forenoon on his calculations.

Aug. 29th (Third Day) All hands up early this morning; had breakfast; we all took a wash in the stream.

A signal pole was put in position, and the place called Castle as it resembled a castle; the rocks were in squares as if laid out.

Mr. Hunt took observations; the boat was put in readiness and launched. Having a good breeze, we went about five miles an hour, standing out from the land to clear a cape ahead of us. Here we met some heavy ice, and did some fine steering to keep clear of it. Hundreds of walrus were seen around here; we fired at some on the ice, but had very few good shots among us, so didn't hit any of them. We ran in toward the shore, and saw animals about the size of dogs, running along the beach—supposed they were foxes, as we afterward saw a great many on shore.

We stood out again for the cape. It was very low land; looking inland, we could see many high mountains of a yellow tint, looking like mountains of gold. Now we have met heavier ice, and found a tide running about two miles an hour from the cape we were heading for. We got some cheese and biscuit for dinner. It was very cold; when we got within a mile of the cape from a bay there came drifting heavy ice, moving about four miles and hour. The bay was on the other side of the cape. Here we saw a red and black fox on the beach.

Took in sail to land, and, while taking in sail, drifted half a mile; had to use a white ash breeze to get to the beach. The boat was pulled up, and a fire lit; while dinner was being . . . . [page 212 missing from the MS] . . . .close to him, but here he slept till supper had been cooked and eaten. After supper Mr. Zane went to have a wash, and found a river near where we were. It was decided that we camp at the river, and, as we could not move the river to where the boat was, we cut a channel for the boat, hauled her through, and brought all the stuff here. Set up the tent; it was taken down and set up again, under Mr. Hunt's special directions; the fire was brought to the door of the tent. Some stood watch, the rest of us turned in. This camp place we called Zane's River.

Aug. 31st (Fifth Day) Broke camp, and got to sea early this morning, but a stiff breeze was blowing, and we got in the leeward of some ice and were fast drifting with it. This fact did not affect Mr. Hunt; he didn't pull in hard weather. Again we started for another piece of ice; after eight hours' hard pulling, eating only a few hard tack and some cheese, and working the boat through the ice, trying to make a landing, we finally pulled under a little bluff. Here we found a small stream of water, afterwards found a skull; some thought it looked like a human skull.

The boat was hauled up in the stream and anchored; tent put up; had supper; stood usual watch; called the place Skeleton Camp.

Sept. 1ˢᵗ (Sixth Day) All hands up early this morning. It was quite cold; we had breakfast, loaded the boat; all on board, and we started. We pulled a long while, then got out on the beach and towed her in smooth water until we came to a lot of level land, with a stream running through it, in and out with the tide. We rested here, had dinner and hard tack; put up land mark and took observations; got to sea and pulled till five P.M. We went on shore, hauled up and discharged the boat; we put up the tent, and had to put guys on it to keep the heavy wind from blowing it over. The boat was turned over and copper patches put on the bottom; we stood watch in turns, and camped here for the night.

Sept. 2ⁿᵈ (Seventh Day) This morning it commenced raining. We got to sea early, and commenced pulling; then had a head wind, and had to beat against it till about noon. We made to shore, cooked dinner; got to sea again, beating in the rain that was fast falling; out oars again, and we pulled until we came to a small lake, which was alive with ducks as far as we could see. We tried to enter this lake, but only found one foot of water. While we were paddling about it became so misty that we could not see the land. Then we tacked again for the land, and got aground on the beach, right under the big hill. We got the boat afloat again, and stood off shore for an hour; we then headed for the shore again, and got aground in one foot of water. We could see about fifteen land spits all around us. Our navigator was bothered for a long time, and swore some; when it cleared up he could see where we were. The heavy ice was about ten miles away aground. Finally, we camped on the nearest spit. The closer we got to shore, the deeper the water was. We lit a big fire to cook supper and dry clothes; pitched tent; turned in; no watch stood.

Sept. 3ʳᵈ (Eighth Day) Broke camp, and loaded the boat early this morning; had a good breeze at starting; met heavy iced; had to take in sail and use paddles for a while. Put up sail again till about noon; had lunch in the afternoon. It commenced to snow, and the wind died out. We could not get close to the beach on account of the ice in shore. Finally, we had to head back where we started from our last campground. We got here all wet through; landed and hauled up the boat; lit a big fire to dry our clothes. On this sand spit, the men found some walrus tusks that were brought back to the ship. The tent was put up; had supper; turned in; no watch.

Sept 4th (Ninth Day) Mist and snow this morning when we broke camp. Loaded the boat and got to sea again. Before starting had a good breakfast of bear tongue. Stood off from the sand spit, and, on account of fog, had to run in to land again. The boat was hauled in and unloaded; the tent was put up. While supper was cooking the men walked for a few miles along the coast. They saw nothing of importance, and came back; had all night in; no watch stood. Observations taken here, and land marks put up.

Sept 5th (Tenth Day) This morning we got up early. It was Mr. Hunt's intention to start back if he couldn't see a lead ahead. This morning we commenced hauling the boat in the shallow water, along the beach; then had to paddle through the ice. At two P.M. as the given time for going from the ship was used up, we put about and started for home. During the afternoon, the boat had some narrow escapes in moving through the ice. When evening came we landed below the camp ground on the spit; men tired and glad to be returning. No watch.

Sept. 6th (Eleventh Day) This morning we made a very early start; after breakfast loaded the boat, and got off. There was ice all around. Commenced by hauling the boat along, then working the paddles and oars when we could. The water, for a long time, was shallow, only about one foot. Most of the things that would float we put overboard and towed, including the bearskin. Didn't stop for dinner; had the hardest day's work since we came out, and kept at it till after midnight. Then had to melt snow to cook coffee; at one the next morning we turned in; no watch stood.

Sept. 7th (Twelfth Day) On account of the hard work of yesterday, we slept late, and did not get away this morning till after nine; then we put up landmark and started. Pulled along till noon, then sailed till seven P.M. when we saw the beach and steered for it. We landed here; it was the first spit we had camped on.

Mr. Hunt told us which was the most northern point of Wrangel Island, and proposes to call the place after a friend of his, if Captain Berry will allow it.

Here we put up the tent and camped, melting show to cook with. All night in; no watch. This place is near Sugar Loaf Mountain.

Sept. 8th (Thirteenth Day) Up early this morning; put up a large pole with all the names of the party in an empty Condensed Milk can. Had breakfast, then launched and put to sea. Had a fine breeze at starting; passed some of our old camp grounds. At noon had lunch of sardines and hard tack. Sailed till five P.M., then met heavy ice and many small fish on which thousands of sea-gulls were feeding. We commenced to shoot at the gulls, and killed a few. Went on shore; about 6 P.M. lit a big fire to dry our clothes. Put up tent; set fox traps, then turned in. Carpenter's mate fixed boat before turning in.

This camp was about one mile from Zane's River.

Sept. 9th (Fourteenth Day) Got ready early, and shortly after daylight got to sea. Made sail; had a good breeze; met heavy ice where we least expected it, but kept on working through it, and, at 4 P.M. reached Fox Point. There was lots of driftwood; when we landed a big fire was built, as we had to dry our clothes. The tent was put up, and we had quite a good supper.

At night took observations of the moon. Saw the Northern lights as one sees them only in these northern latitudes. No watch; saw bear's den and foxes.

Sept. 10th (Fifteenth Day) Up early for a start this morning; went through the usual routine. There was no wind when we started, so we pulled till about half way between Foxes' Point and Castle Don. Here we went in shore among the big pieces of ice that had been driven up on the beach; the boat was hauled up and the tent put in a good place; had supper, dried clothes and turned in; no watch.

Sept 11th (Sixteenth Day) We had a visitor this morning that woke us up. A big Polar Bear came and looked into the tent; some one hollers out, "A bear!" All hands up, and a rush was made for rifles. We had not used the rifles much, and being in the weather, they were not in a very good condition. Before we could get around to have a shot at him, Mr. Bear was out of range. The excitement gave us an appetite; we cooked and ate breakfast, then put to sea. Met heavy ice, with lots of walrus—thousands of them seen here, and we met them during all the trip in great numbers. We shot at them, but failed to get any. We had now all we could do to work through the ice with the paddles, trying to make a landing near where we shot the bear. Again, at the beach the heavy ice gave us great trouble. The tide was coming in, and we had to carry the boat and stuff far in from the water.

We were not at a point about three miles from where the bear was killed. When we came out we pitched ten, cooked and ate supper; lit a big fire to dry clothes. Stood no watch; hoped to make the ship next day; turned in.

Sept 12th (Seventeenth Day) In the morning we were all anxious to be on board of the ship this night, so made an early start. Before leaving, put a lot of empty shells on the beach for a landmark, as big wood was scarce. We then put to sea, and came to where the river was, at Bear Point. Here we landed, and one of the men went to look for the bear's carcass. It was almost gone, other animals having eaten it. The tracks of bears and foxes were plainly seen.

We had a sailor's dinner—hard tack, soup and boalee. All the sugar, coffee, peaches, and other good eating gave out. We did hunt up a few boxes of sardines.

We put to sea again; got a good breeze that carried us to the ship; had to beat part of the way. As we came alongside the men cheered us.

Mr. Hunt told the men not to say anything about the bear, but Johansen yelled out, "I shot a bear!"

We got on board; all well; found the others had all got back. Men were charged with the clothes they had to use on this trip.

I am indebted to Edward O'Leary, First-class Fireman, and others of the party for their account of Mr. Hunt's trip.

[Here ends the transcription of Patrick Cahill's manuscript.]

# # #

Glossary

Belvedere:: A whaler, and sister ship to the *Rodgers*, according to Cahill entry September 27, 1881.

Black Fish: In Cahill's usage here, most likely genus Globicephalus, which goes about in shoals that often enter harbors.

Boalee: [reference unknown]

Books saved from the fire:
   Asphodel
   Bound to the Wheel
   Jacob Faithful by Frederick Marryat
   Lakeside Novels
   Lalla Rookh (1817) an oriental romance by Thomas Moore
   Owen Meredith's Poems
   Moths
   "*Moody*" and "*Sanky*" Hymn Books
   Pirate's Book
   Popinjay
   Squire's Legacy (1875) by Mary Cecil Hay
   Swedenborg's Works

Dinghy: A small wooden ship's boat propelled by oars, much smaller than a whaler (whaleboat), launch, or lifeboat.

Forecastle, as used on board ships like the *Rodgers:* By tradition the men's quarters were in the fo'c'sle (forecastle), the narrow quarters in the very bow of the ship, forward of the foremost mast. Even in later ships with more modern accommodations, the men's quarters continued to be known as the fo'c'sle, wherever in the ship it happened to be located.

Fox Islands and *Ouniac Island* are in the Aleutian Archipelago, nearer to the mainland.

Gam: When two or more whaling ships are hove-to in the same area, the men and officers will visit each others' ships for a pleasant change of company.

Hulo hulo: A native dance. Cahill is using a variant spelling of "hula hula."

Jenny Legs: [Reference unknown]

Kuchanka: A deerskin robe.

Kuklanka: A storm coat.

Maskinka: A native of Masinka Bay. Also used as a general reference to the inhabitants of the vicinity of St. Lawrence Bay.

Mukee: Kill, or murder.

Pirogans:: Cahill is probably referring to "broghans," using the gaelic word for a heavy laced usually ankle-high work boot generically for a locally made footgear.

Plover Bay: A whaler's cove near the eastern extremity of Siberia.

Putnam's Island: Another name for the winter station set out at Cape Sergkaman by the *Rodger* on her return from Wrangel Island.

Sailor's Blessing: A spirited outpouring of blasphemous, profane, often scatological oaths in response to some particularly trying circumstance.

Shantee: A variant spelling for "chantey," a sailor's work-song used to coordinate the pulling of lines when raising sail or doing other heavy work requiring many hands. These were commonly used on deck in the merchant service, and forbidden on most naval ships.

Sculpin: A fish, generically used here, but elsewhere any small freshwater fish having a large head with small spines on each side.

"Sent to the mast" or *"Sent forward"*: Disrated. An officer or petty officer, when demoted from his position, was "sent forward" to take up his new station among "the men."

Settlements and geographical locales:
   Akuneen
   Cape Sergkaman (present day Cape Serdze)
   Indian Head
   Kalucien Bay
   Lerene
   Maskinka Bay: Inlet a few miles north of Plover Bay.
   North Head and *South Head* (at the entrance to St. Lawrence Bay)
   Nutarin (largest native settlement near St. Lawrence Bay)
   Nutapinmen
   Putnam's Island: Present-day Tiapka Island off Cape Serdze, where Mr. Putnam established his winter base. St. Lawrence Bay, where the ship burned and her crew stranded, was about 100 miles to the southeast.
   Seneen (or Seeneen)
   Yandanghai (South Head)

Sealskin rope: The hide of a seal carcase would be cut in very long narrow continuous strips many yards long around its circumference. These strips would then be plaited into a very strong and flexible line used with harpoons in future seal hunts.

Swing Ship: At sea, a ship's compass must also be corrected for errors, called deviation, caused by iron and steel in its structure and equipment. The ship is *swung*, that is rotated about a fixed point while its heading is noted by alignment with fixed points on the shore.

Trade stuff: Various articles—needles, steel for knives, calico, fishhooks, and the like—that are of little value back in the states, but which could be traded with the natives for fur clothing, food, artifacts of various kinds to be sold for a nice profit at home.

Tuck or *tucker*: A derivative of British English slang *tuck* 'consume food or drink'

White ash breeze:: To propel the boat by oar, commonly made from the wood of the white ash tree.

Yarat: Outer hut, or porch. This is where the dogs lived.

Yoronger: The native word for house or home. The Tchoutkichi people lived in domed huts made of walrus skin.

About Terra Nova Press:

This small POD publishing enterprise seeks to bring into print the smaller, less-well-known true stories of polar exploration in the days of the sailing ships. We are actively seeking unpublished first-hand accounts for publication, with a view to making them available readers and historians of the Arctic and Antarctic.

About the editor:

David Hirzel's lifelong studies of Arctic and Antarctic exploration and discovery have resulted in two books on the Irish sailor Tom Crean's adventures with Scott and Shackleton in the Antarctic, as well as two short plays based on events in the Franklin expeditions. He currently makes his home at Sky Ranch overlooking the Pacific Ocean at Pacifica CA.

Acknowledgments:

I am greatly indebted to Sue Proudfoot for offering me the opportunity to bring her great-grandfather Patrick Cahill's book into publication for a wider audience. The preparation of his manuscript for print has been edifying and humbling. I here offer my grateful appreciation to Gina Bardi, Research Librarian at the J. Porter Shaw Library of the San Francisco Maritime National Historical Park, who located the photographs used in this book, and to that library for its gracious permission to use them; to my sister Nancy and to my dear Alice Cochran, who have supported me in my sometimes extravagant dreams of adding something meaningful to the canon of polar literature; to Maureen Cutajar, conjures my typescript drafts into print-ready formats; and for fact-checking, to our generous Margie Navarro.

Photographs:

The photographs in between Chapters Eight and Nine in this book are used by permission from the J. Porter Shaw Library of the San Francisco Maritime National Historical Park.